ACTION PHILOSOPHERS

Fred Van Lente & Ryan Dunlavey

 ™ Rocketship Entertainment, LLC
rocketshipent.com

Tom Akel, CEO & Publisher • **Rob Feldman,** CTO • **Jeanmarie McNeely,** CFO
Brandon Freeberg, Dir. of Campaign Mgmt. • **Phil Smith,** Art Director • **Aram Alekyan,** Designer
Jimmy Deoquino, Designer • **Jed Keith,** Social Media • **Jerrod Clark,** Publicity

Action Philosophers volume 2 Omnipotence For Dummies
Softcover Edition ISBN: 978-1-962298-13-1 | Hardcover Edition ISBN: 978-1-962298-14-8

ACT

PHILOS

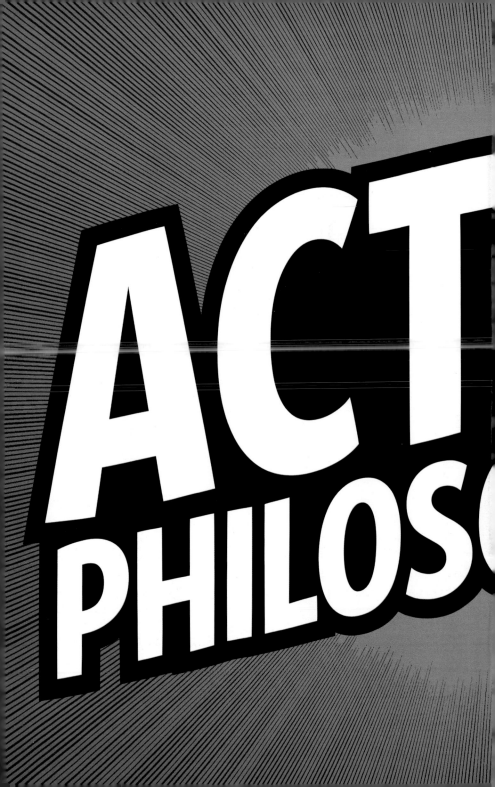

ION

OPHERS

OMNIPOTENCE FOR DUMMIES

FRED VAN LENTE - writer
RYAN DUNLAVEY - artist
ADAM GUZOWSKI - colorist

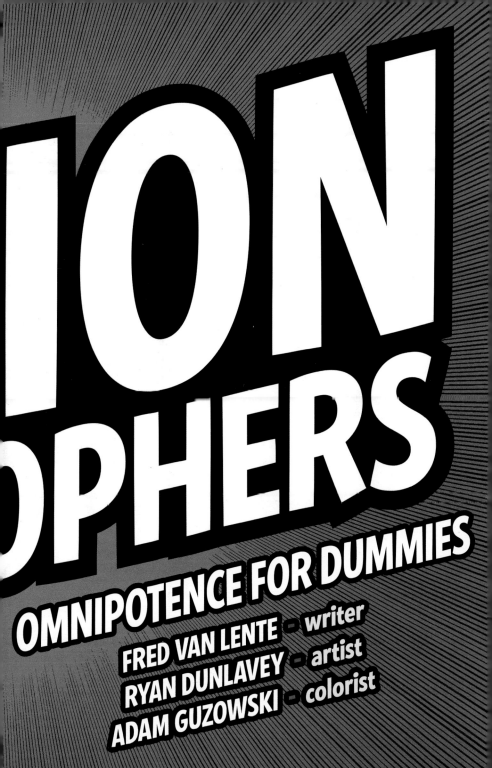

TABLE OF CONTENTS

GOD MODE

The Empiricism Strikes Back

Politically Correct

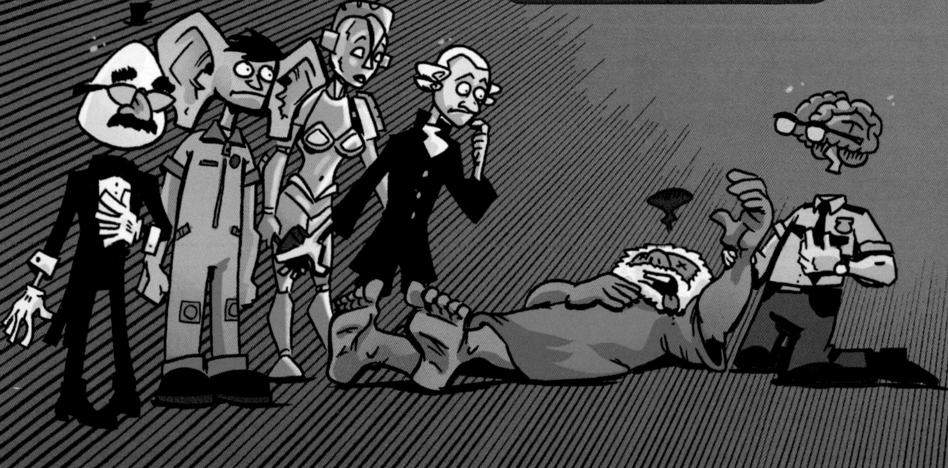

"Philosophy is not a **theory**, but an **activity**."

-Ludwig Wittgenstein
Tractatus Logico-Philosophicus

LADIES AND GENTS! WITHOUT FURTHER ADIEU, WE'RE PROUD TO PRESENT THE *FATHER* OF MODERN PHILOSOPHY...

ACTION PHILOSOPHER #13...

RENÉ DESCARTES!

FRED VAN LENTE *WRITES* & RYAN DUNLAVEY *DRAWS,* THEREFORE THEY *ARE!*

RENÉ?

RENNY-BABY?

C'MON OUT AND KNOCK 'EM DEAD, SON!

I'M OVER *HERE.*

UH ... THEN WHY DON'T YOU COME *OUT?* W-WE GOT ⸝HEH⸝ *PAYING CUSTOMERS* WHO SLAPPED DOWN *GOOD MONEY* FOR THIS HERE *PHILOSOPHY COMIC...*

...AND THE *SHOW MUST GO ON,* TO COIN A CLICHE! ⸝HEH!⸝

IT'S JUST... THERE'S A *SLIGHT PROBLEM...*

1

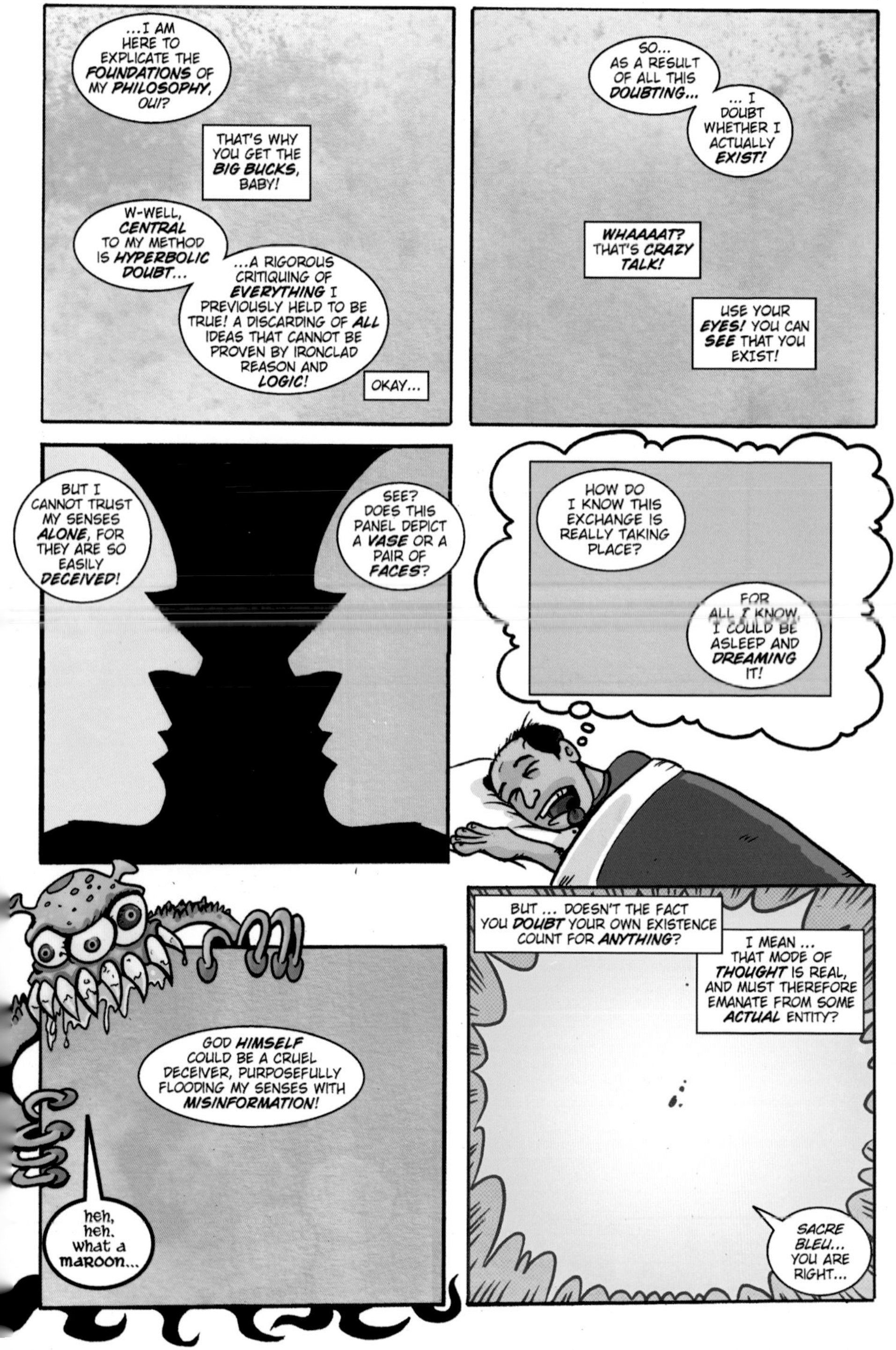
...I AM HERE TO EXPLICATE THE FOUNDATIONS OF MY PHILOSOPHY, OUI?
THAT'S WHY YOU GET THE BIG BUCKS, BABY!
W-WELL, CENTRAL TO MY METHOD IS HYPERBOLIC DOUBT...
...A RIGOROUS CRITIQUING OF EVERYTHING I PREVIOUSLY HELD TO BE TRUE! A DISCARDING OF ALL IDEAS THAT CANNOT BE PROVEN BY IRONCLAD REASON AND LOGIC!
OKAY...
SO... AS A RESULT OF ALL THIS DOUBTING...
... I DOUBT WHETHER I ACTUALLY EXIST!
WHAAAAT? THAT'S CRAZY TALK!
USE YOUR EYES! YOU CAN SEE THAT YOU EXIST!
BUT I CANNOT TRUST MY SENSES ALONE, FOR THEY ARE SO EASILY DECEIVED!
SEE? DOES THIS PANEL DEPICT A VASE OR A PAIR OF FACES?
HOW DO I KNOW THIS EXCHANGE IS REALLY TAKING PLACE?
FOR ALL I KNOW, I COULD BE ASLEEP AND DREAMING IT!
GOD HIMSELF COULD BE A CRUEL DECEIVER, PURPOSEFULLY FLOODING MY SENSES WITH MISINFORMATION!
heh, heh. what a maroon...
BUT ... DOESN'T THE FACT YOU DOUBT YOUR OWN EXISTENCE COUNT FOR ANYTHING?
I MEAN ... THAT MODE OF THOUGHT IS REAL, AND MUST THEREFORE EMANATE FROM SOME ACTUAL ENTITY?
SACRE BLEU... YOU ARE RIGHT...

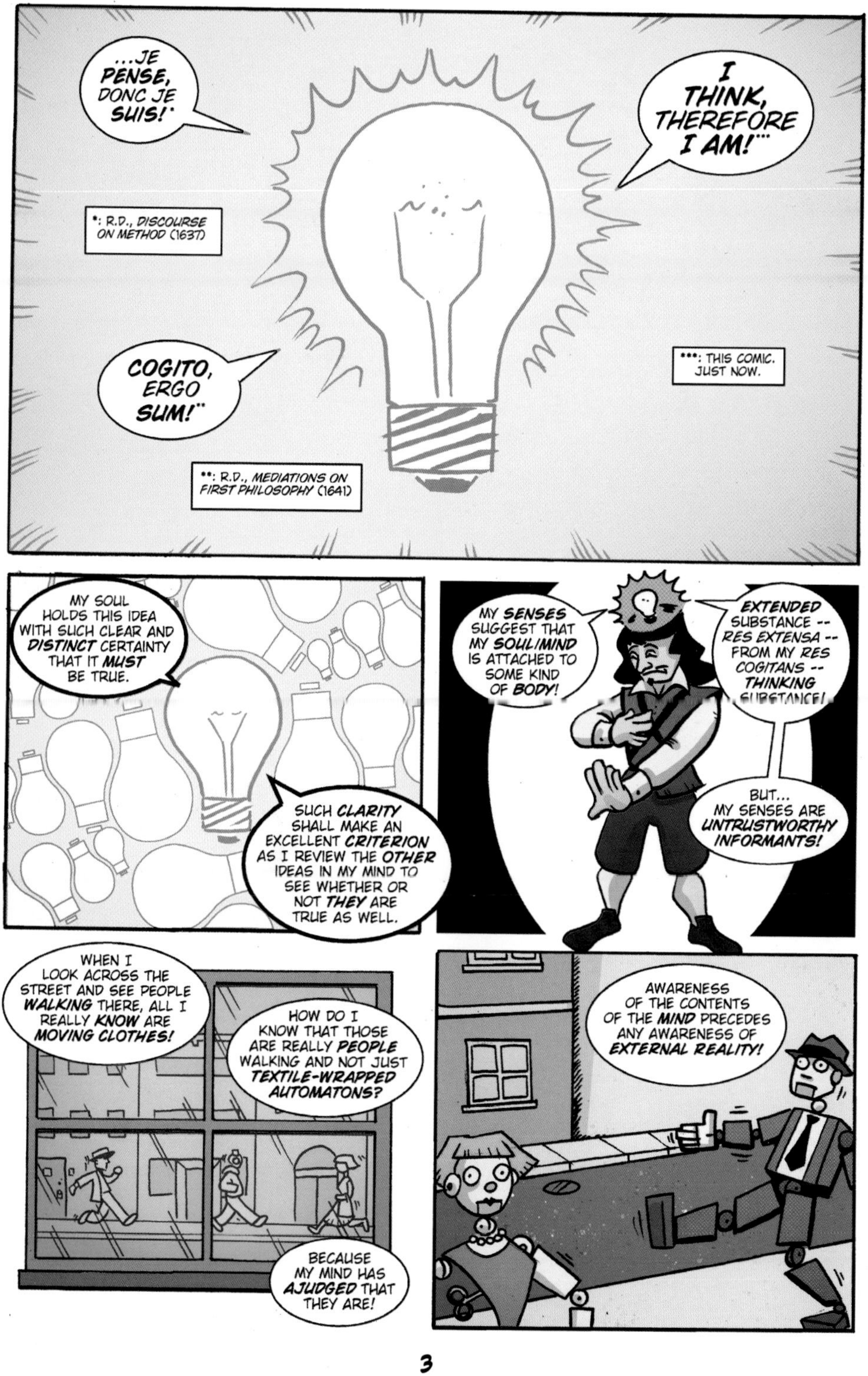
...JE PENSE, DONC JE SUIS!*
I THINK, THEREFORE I AM!***
*: R.D., DISCOURSE ON METHOD (1637)
COGITO, ERGO SUM!**
***: THIS COMIC. JUST NOW.
**: R.D., MEDIATIONS ON FIRST PHILOSOPHY (1641)
MY SOUL HOLDS THIS IDEA WITH SUCH CLEAR AND DISTINCT CERTAINTY THAT IT MUST BE TRUE.
SUCH CLARITY SHALL MAKE AN EXCELLENT CRITERION AS I REVIEW THE OTHER IDEAS IN MY MIND TO SEE WHETHER OR NOT THEY ARE TRUE AS WELL.
MY SENSES SUGGEST THAT MY SOUL/MIND IS ATTACHED TO SOME KIND OF BODY!
EXTENDED SUBSTANCE -- RES EXTENSA -- FROM MY RES COGITANS -- THINKING SUBSTANCE!
BUT... MY SENSES ARE UNTRUSTWORTHY INFORMANTS!
WHEN I LOOK ACROSS THE STREET AND SEE PEOPLE WALKING THERE, ALL I REALLY KNOW ARE MOVING CLOTHES!
HOW DO I KNOW THAT THOSE ARE REALLY PEOPLE WALKING AND NOT JUST TEXTILE-WRAPPED AUTOMATONS?
BECAUSE MY MIND HAS AJUDGED THAT THEY ARE!
AWARENESS OF THE CONTENTS OF THE MIND PRECEDES ANY AWARENESS OF EXTERNAL REALITY!

AN INVENTORY OF MY MIND'S **CONTENTS** REVEALS THREE DISTINCT **TYPES** OF IDEAS:

FICTITIOUS IDEAS, WHICH THE MIND **INVENTS**...

....**ADVENTITIOUS** IDEAS, WHICH THE MIND **RECEIVES** FROM THE **EXTERNAL WORLD**...

....AND **INATE** IDEAS, WHICH ARE BORN **WITH** THE MIND!

IRONICALLY, THE ONLY CATEGORY I CAN BE **SURE** EXISTS IS **FICTION**, SINCE IT PRESUPPOSES THE EXISTENCE OF MY **MIND** (WHICH IS **ALL** I HAVE PROVEN EXISTS)!

HAW! SUCK MY ION-DRIVE **WAKE**, DENIZEN OF **NON-FICTION**!

AW.

IN ORDER FOR **ADVENTITIOUS** IDEAS TO BE REAL, THEY HAVE TO EXIST **INDEPENDENTLY** OF MY OWN **WILLPOWER**!

BONK!

I CANNOT **WILL** THIS WALL TO **DISAPPEAR**, SO IT IS POSSIBLE THAT IT EXISTS **INDEPENDENTLY** FROM MY MIND!

IF AN IDEA WAS PLACED INTO MY MIND FROM **OUTSIDE** OF ME, THE CAUSE **MUST** HAVE AS MUCH **REALITY** AS I CONCEIVE TO BE IN THE WALL **ITSELF**!

BONK!

TRADITIONALLY, THIS IS KNOWN AS THE **PRINCIPLE** OF **SUFFICIENT REASON**!

FOR EXAMPLE, I HOLD AN IDEA OF A **GOD** THAT IS **INFINITELY PERFECT**...

I AM **AWESOME**!

...AND THAT IDEA COULD **ONLY** HAVE BEEN PLANTED BY SOMETHING THAT **IS** INFINITELY PERFECT!

REPORT CARD

MATH — A+∞
CIENCE- A+∞
STORY- A+∞
ART- A+∞
GYM — A+∞
CONDUCT- A+∞

4

NOR CAN A **CAUSE** CREATE AN EFFECT THAT IS **MORE PERFECT** THAN ITSELF!

(EVEN THOUGH I CAN IMAGINE THE **FICTITIOUS** IDEA OF THE **"PERFECT WOMAN,"** I CANNOT **ACTUALIZE** THE PERFECT WOMAN MYSELF!)

SIGH... BACK TO THE **DRAWING BOARD**...

IT FOLLOWS, THEN, THAT FALLIBLE, FINITE **ME** COULD ONLY HAVE BEEN CAUSED BY A **PERFECT, INFINITE** SOURCE!

IN OTHER WORDS, **I** EXIST--

--THEREFORE, **GOD EXISTS!**

(THOUGH IT IS **THEORETICALLY POSSIBLE** I COULD HAVE BEEN CREATED BY A CAUSE **EQUAL** TO ME...

...**THAT** FINITE, FALLIBLE CAUSE WOULD HAVE THE IDEA OF THE INFINITE PERFECT **AS WELL**, WHICH MUST HAVE BEEN IMPLANTED BY AN INFINITELY PERFECT SOURCE!)

APPROVED BY INSPECTOR

OUR **INNATE IDEA** OF THE INFINITELY PERFECT **GOD** IS THE MARK OF THE **CRAFTSMAN** STAMPED ON HIS WORK!

IF GOD IS **PERFECT**, IT FOLLOWS THAT HE IS NOT A **DECEIVER!**

ONE **DISSEMBLES** ONLY TO PROTECT **VULNERABILITIES**, WHICH A **PERFECT** BEING WOULD NOT **HAVE!**

AND SINCE **GOD** CREATED MY SENSES, MEMORY, AND OTHER INTELLECTUAL FACULTIES, AND SINCE HE IS NOT A **DECEIVER...**

...THEN MY **SENSES**, ON THE WHOLE, CAN BE **TRUSTED!**

5

YET THIS ALLEGED *"EXTERNAL WORLD"* (WHICH I HAVE NOT YET PROVEN *EXISTS*) EVIDENCES TWO VERY *DIFFERENT* SETS OF PROPERTIES!

MY *EYES* TELL ME THE SUN IS VERY *SMALL*, AND THE SENSATION OF *HEAT* ON MY *SKIN* SUGGESTS IT IS VERY *CLOSE BY!*

BUT MY *MIND* KNOWS THAT THIS IS *NOT TRUE!* ASTRONOMICAL AND MATHEMATICAL DATA SHOW THAT THE SUN IS BOTH VERY *BIG* AND VERY *FAR AWAY!*

THESE *INHERENT* FACTORS OF THE SUN'S BEING-- VOLUME AND DISTANCE --ARE ITS *PRIMARY PROPERTIES!* AND DERIVING FROM THOSE ARE *SECONDARY* PROPERTIES SUCH AS COLOR AND ODOR!

ALL THINGS, BUT ESPECIALLY *ME*, ARE SPLIT BETWEEN THESE PRIMARY AND SECONDARY PROPERTIES!

THUS THE *MIND* AND THE *BODY* ARE TWO *RADICALLY* DIFFERENT ENTITIES--WE HUMANS ARE INHERENTLY *DUALISTIC!*

SINCE MY SENSES ARE PART OF MY *BODY* AND NOT OF MY MIND, I CANNOT BE CREATING THESE STIMULI *MYSELF* (*I.E.*, THROUGH *INVENTED* IDEAS).

GOD COULD NOT BE *FEEDING* THESE SECONDARY PROPERTIES DIRECTLY *TO ME*, SINCE WE HAVE ESTABLISHED THAT HE IS NOT A *DECEIVER.*

HOKUM

NOR COULD I BE *DREAMING* THESE SECONDARY PROPERTIES, FOR *MEMORY* TIES THE EVENTS OF OUR WAKING LIVES *TOGETHER.*

(IN A *DREAM* I DO NOT REMEMBER *ALL* THE DREAMS I HAD BEFORE *THAT* ONE.)

I REMEMBER *ALL* OF MY LIFE UP UNTIL THIS POINT, SO I MUST BE *AWAKE!*

THEREFORE... I HAVE NO OTHER *CHOICE* BUT TO CONCLUDE...

...THAT I RECEIVE PASSIVE PERCEPTIONS OF AN *EXTERNAL WORLD*...

...BECAUSE AN EXTERNAL WORLD ACTUALLY *EXISTS!*

DESCARTES HIT UPON HIS REVOLUTIONARY METHODOLOGY WHILE SERVING IN THE *THIRTY YEARS WAR.*

IN NOVEMBER 1619 HE FOUND HIMSELF STUCK IN A *SNOWBOUND* LITTLE ROOM IN *NEUBERG,* GERMANY.

LITTLE WONDER HIS MIND SOON TURNED TOWARD *PHILOSOPHICAL PURSUITS.*

SOOOOO BOOOOORRRED...

HEY...I WONDER IF IT'D EVER BE POSSIBLE FOR *ALL* HUMAN KNOWLEDGE TO ATTAIN THE PRECISE ACCURACY OF *MATHEMATICS?*

THAT EVENING, THE YOUNG SOLDIER HAD A *DREAM* THAT CONVINCED HIM THAT *GOD* HAD INDEED SHOWN HIM THE CLEAREST PATH TO *TRUTH.*

AS LONG AS THE MIND IS CAREFUL TO AVOID THE *PITFALLS* LAID OUT FOR IT BY THE BODY'S FAULTY PERCEPTIONS...

...*ABSOLUTE KNOWLEDGE* OF ALL THINGS *IS* ATTAINABLE BY *HUMAN REASON!*

DESCARTES APPLIED HIS EXACTING METHOD TO PHYSICS, ASTRONOMY, PSYCHOLOGY, ANATOMY, AND, MOST FAMOUSLY, *MATH.*

NATURE CAN BE DEFINED THROUGH *NUMBERS!*

HIS SYSTEM OF *CARTESIAN COORDINATES* FORMED THE BEDROCK OF *ANALYTICAL GEOMETRY!*

RENE

HE ALSO WROTE A COMPREHENSIVE TREATISE ON *PHYSICS, THE WORLD,* BUT CHANGED HIS MIND ABOUT *PUBLISHING* IT ONCE *GALILEO* WAS PUT ON TRIAL FOR SUPPORTING *SIMILAR* IDEAS.

YOU GOT A *PROBLEM* WITH THAT, FRENCHIE?

WHO, *ME?* >HEH!< ... NON!

7

UNFORTUNATELY FOR *HIM*, HIS FAME REACHED THE ECCENTRIC YOUNG QUEEN OF *SWEDEN*, CHRISTINA.

I HAVE THE BEST OF *EVERYTHING*...

...I WANT THE BEST *PHILOSOPHY TUTOR* TOO! BRING THE FRENCHMAN TO *ME*!

Y-YES, MUM!

CHRISTINA SCHEDULED THEIR SESSIONS FOR *5AM* SHARP, THREE DAYS A WEEK.

A-CHOO! !@#$! *SWEDISH WINTERS*!!

TWO MONTHS INTO HIS NEW JOB, DESCARTES CAUGHT A COLD THAT QUICKLY SNOWBALLED INTO *PNEUMONIA*.

HE STRUGGLED FOR A *WEEK*, THEN DIED ON FEB. 11, 1650...

SPARE THE FRENCH BLOOD! >GAK!<

...AT *4AM*, PERHAPS TO AVOID ANOTHER APPOINTMENT WITH THE *KOOKY QUEEN*!

MANY BELIEVED THAT SINCE DESCARTES HAD *LOGICALLY* PROVEN GOD'S EXISTENCE, HE WOULD BE A *SHOO-IN* FOR *SAINTHOOD*!

AS HIS BODY WAS TRANSPORTED BACK TO *FRANCE*, OVER-EAGER PILGRIMS PICKED APART THE CORPSE FOR *RELICS*!

FRANCE

LOOK, MA! I GOT THE *DRUMSTICK*! AYUK!

ONE OF THE MOST *REVERED* FIGURES IN FRENCH HISTORY, DESCARTES WAS LAID TO REST AT THE CATHEDRAL OF *ST.-GERMAIN-DES-PRÉS* IN PARIS'S *LATIN QUARTER*...

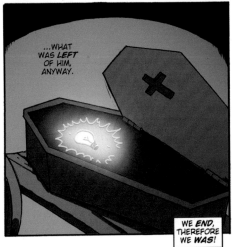

...WHAT WAS *LEFT* OF HIM, ANYWAY.

WE *END*, THEREFORE WE *WAS*!

Baruch Spinoza

(1632-1677) HAD A POETICALLY APPROPRIATE **DAY JOB** FOR A PHILOSOPHER...

...HE CRAFTED GLASS LENSES FOR **TELESCOPES**, SO THE **HEAVENS** MIGHT BE BETTER **VIEWED**.

BORN INTO A PROSPEROUS JEWISH **MERCANTILE** FAMILY, SPINOZA SHOULD HAVE ENJOYED A MUCH MORE **LUXURIOUS** LIFESTYLE THAN THAT OF HUMBLE **ARTISAN**.

UNFORTUNATELY, SOME OF THE **NOSIER** MEMBERS OF HIS AMSTERDAM TEMPLE HAD HEARD **RUMORS** ABOUT THE CONCLUSIONS SPINOZA HAD REACHED IN HIS AMATEUR **PHILOSOPHICAL** WRITINGS.

COME NOW, BENTO, TELL US YOUR **REAL** VIEWS. YOU CAN **TRUST** US. ARE WE NOT YOUR **FRIENDS**?

IF ONE READS THE **TALMUD**, IT WOULD SEEM THE SOUL IS NOT **IMMORTAL**--THAT THERE ARE **NO ANGELS**--AND THAT GOD HAS A **CORPOREAL BODY**.

BARELY **TWENTY-FOUR** YEARS OLD, SPINOZA HAD NOT YET LEARNED THE VALUE OF **CAUTION** OVER **PRIDE**.

"I CONFESS THAT SINCE **NOTHING** IS TO BE FOUND IN THE BIBLE ABOUT THE IMMATERIAL OR INCORPOREAL, THERE IS NOTHING **OBJECTIONABLE** IN BELIEVING THAT GOD IS A BODY."

"ALL THE **MORE** SO SINCE, AS IT SAYS IN PSALMS (48:1), 'GOD IS **GREAT**,' AND IT IS **IMPOSSIBLE** TO COMPREHEND GREATNESS WITHOUT **EXTENSION**, AND, THEREFORE, WITH-OUT **BODY**."

SPINOZA SPOKE OF OTHER *HERETICAL* THINGS -- THAT THE EXISTENCE OF *ANGELS* AND OTHER SPIRITS AND THE IMMORTALITY OF THE *SOUL* CANNOT BE JUSTIFIED BY *SCRIPTURE*.

HE REALIZED HE *OVERSPOKE* WHEN AN UNKNOWN ASSASSIN TRIED TO *STAB* HIM AS HE LEFT TEMPLE!

BENTO *KEPT* THE COAT FROM THAT DAY WITH HIM, TEAR AND ALL...

...PERHAPS TO REMIND HIM THAT THE LIFE OF THE *MIND* IS NOT ALWAYS THE *PEACEFUL* LIFE!

DUTCH JEWS WERE IN AN *ODD* POSITION IN THE MID-1600s. HOLLAND HAD AGREED TO TAKE THEM IN AFTER SPAIN'S *KING FERDINAND* EXPELLED THEM FROM THE IBERIAN PENINSULA (SPINOZA'S FAMILY WAS ETHNICALLY *PORTUGUESE*) ONLY SO LONG AS THEY DIDN'T STIR UP *RELIGIOUS* TROUBLE.

EUROPEAN *CHRISTIANS* HAD ENOUGH PROBLEMS OF THEIR *OWN* WITH THE BLOODY PROTESTANT/CATHOLIC SCHISM WITHOUT SHOULDERING THE BLASPHEMIES OF *OTHER* FAITHS.

AMSTERDAM'S RABBIS HAD ASSUMED THAT, AS SPINOZA WAS SUCH A *LEARNED* YOUTH, HE WAS ALSO *PIOUS*.

WAAA! BENTO SAID WE'RE NOT *IMMORTAL*!

AND HE DOUBTS MOSES WROTE THE WHOLE *TORAH*! WAAA!

HIS *ENEMIES* SOON CONVINCED THEM *OTHERWISE*.

HAULED BEFORE THE LEADERS OF DUTCH JEWRY, SPINOZA WAS OFFERED THE AWESOME SUM OF *ONE THOUSAND GUILDERS* TO PUBLICLY *RECANT*.

HIS *REPLY*?

"IN RETURN FOR THE TROUBLE YOU HAVE TAKEN TO TEACH ME THE *HEBREW LANGUAGE*, I AM QUITE WILLING TO SHOW YOU HOW TO *EXCOMMUNICATE* ME."*

*: ACTUAL QUOTE!

10

JEWS AREN'T REALLY THE EXCOMMUNICATING *TYPE*, BUT SPINOZA MANAGED TO REALLY *PISS OFF* THE RABBIS. THEY ELECTED TO MAKE AN *EXAMPLE* OF HIM.

ON JULY 27, 1656, A WRIT OF *CHERUM* WAS READ ALOUD BEFORE THE ARK OF AMSTERDAM:

DE-JEW 8000 xl

"THE SAID SPINOZA SHOULD BE EXCOMMUNICATED AND *EXPELLED* FROM THE PEOPLE OF *ISRAEL*..."

"...THE ANGER OF THE LORD AND HIS *JEALOUSY* SHALL SMOKE *AGAINST* THAT MAN, AND ALL THE *CURSES* THAT ARE WRITTEN IN THIS BOOK SHALL LIE UPON HIM, AND THE LORD SHALL *BLOT OUT HIS NAME* FROM UNDER *HEAVEN*."

Spinoza DRY GOODS

100% OFF!

THE *CHERUM* ALSO FORBADE ANY JEW FROM COMING WITHIN *SIX FEET* OF HIM ... SO SPINOZA HAD TO GET OUT OF THE *MERCHANT* GAME!

OPTICS WERE THE *CUTTING-EDGE TECH* OF THE 17TH CENTURY...(THE TELESCOPE HAD JUST BEEN *INVENTED* BY A DUTCH EYEGLASS MAKER IN *1600*.)...KIND OF LIKE WHAT *COMPUTER PROGRAMMING* IS TODAY. SO IT'S NO SURPRISE A *BIG BRAIN* LIKE SPINOZA GRAVITATED TOWARD THAT AS A SECOND CAREER.

IN THE ENSUING DECADES SPENT REFINING *GLASS*, SPINOZA WOULD ALSO REFINE HIS *IDEAS* INTO TWO GREAT WORKS, THE *TRACTATUS THEOLOGICO-POLITICUS* AND *ETHICS*.

HEAVILY INFLUENCED BY THE *STOICS*, SPINOZA TOLD A FRIEND:

"I DO NOT DIFFERENTIATE BETWEEN *GOD* AND *NATURE* IN THE WAY THAT ALL THOSE KNOWN TO ME HAVE DONE."

GOD

HIS FORMULATION WAS *DEUS SIVE NATURA*--"GOD OR NATURE"--SIX OF ONE, HALF DOZEN OF THE OTHER!

AS THE NATURE OF A *CIRCLE*, FOR EXAMPLE, LIES IN ITS *ROUNDNESS*...

..."*ALL* THINGS, I SAY, ARE *IN* GOD AND *MOVE* IN GOD."

God

"WHATEVER *IS*, IS *IN* GOD, AND NOTHING CAN EXIST OR BE CONCEIVED *WITHOUT GOD*."

WHAT DROVE THE RABBIS **NUTS** ABOUT SPINOZA WAS HIS INSISTENCE THAT GOD IS NOT A **TRANSITIVE** BUT RATHER AN **IMMANENT** CAUSE OF REALITY.

WRONG!

GOD

THIS VERY **ARISTOTELIAN** DISTINCTION SIMPLY MEANS THAT GOD IS NOT A **PERSONALITY**, OBJECTIVELY **"CREATING"** REALITY LIKE AN ARTISAN CRAFTS A **LENS**.

NO-- GOD CREATES REALITY BY **BEING** REALITY! SPINOZA: "GOD I UNDERSTAND TO BE A BEING ABSOLUTELY **INFINITE**, THAT IS, A SUBSTANCE CONSISTING OF INFINITE ATTRIBUTES, **EACH OF WHICH** EXPRESSES ETERNAL AND INFINITE **ESSENCE**."

EVERYTHING THAT **IS**, THEREFORE, IS MERELY A **"MODE"** OF GOD.

NEW GOD

GOD

GOD ST

GOD

GOD TIMES

RIGHT!

NO **WONDER** SPINOZA'S FELLOW PHILOSOPHERS NICKNAMED HIM "THAT **GOD-INTOXICATED MAN!**"

AWRIGHT, BUDDY, YOU'RE **CUT OFF**.

AND JUST AS A CIRCLE **MUST** BE ROUND, SPINOZA WRITES, "THINGS COULD **NOT** HAVE BEEN PRODUCED BY GOD IN ANY MANNER OR IN ANY ORDER **DIFFERENT** FROM THAT WHICH IN FACT **EXISTS**."

IN THIS WAY SPINOZA **DEMOLISHES** ARISTOTLE'S TWO MILLENNIA-HELD DISTINCTION BETWEEN **POSSIBILITY** AND **ACTUALITY**: IF SOMETHING **COULD** BE, IT **IS**. IF IT **CAN'T**, IT'S **NOT**.

HMMM... SO HARD TO **DECIDE**...

SINCE **FREEDOM** IS NOTHING MORE THAN THE ABILITY TO ACT ACCORDING TO ONE'S OWN **NATURE**, GOD IS ALSO ABSOLUTELY **FREE**.

THEREFORE ... AND THIS IS WHY "THE MAN" **REALLY** CAN'T STAND SPINOZA ... SO ARE **WE**, WHO ARE **PART** OF GOD!

"GOD GIVES NO *LAWS* TO MANKIND SO AS TO *REWARD* THEM WHEN THEY FULFILL THEM AND TO *PUNISH* THEM WHEN THEY TRANSGRESS THEM!"

"OR, TO STATE IT MORE *CLEARLY:*"

"*GOD'S* LAWS ARE NOT OF SUCH NATURE THAT THEY *COULD BE TRANSGRESSED!*"

"MAN IS A PART OF *NATURE* AND MUST FOLLOW *ITS* LAWS..."

"...AND THIS *ALONE* IS *TRUE WORSHIP.*"

PLEASURE IS *NATURE'S* WAY OF POINTING US TOWARD *TRUE* HAPPINESS, AND IT IS *REASON'S* JOB TO CONTROL THE EMOTIONS IN ORDER FOR US TO *SECURE* THAT WHICH MAKES US HAPPY.

PASSIONS--THE EMOTIONS--ARE THE *FUEL* THAT MAKES YOUR LIFE GO, THAT *DRIVES* YOU THROUGH YOUR DAILY *ROUTINE* ...

OOH, *MAMA!* LET'S ASK *HER* OUT!

BUT HOW CAN I GET HER TO *LIKE* ME?

WHO *CARES?* LET'S JUST GO FOR IT!

...BUT *REASON* IS THE *BRAKE* THAT LETS YOU MANAGE AND *MODIFY* YOUR PASSIONS, THAT LETS YOU SET THE BEST *PATH* TO YOUR GOAL, AND UNDERSTAND WHY *SOME* PASSIONS ARE BETTER THAN *OTHERS*.

HERE'S WHAT YOU *DO:* SEND HER A NOTE, BUT DON'T *SIGN* IT; THEN SEND FLOWERS--*ANONYMOUSLY*--TO HER TABLE IN THE CAFERTERIA.

BUILD UP THE IDEA SHE HAS AN *ADMIRER*, THEN WHEN SHE LEAST EXPECTS IT, PSST, PSST...

REASON'S **SECOND** ROLE IS TO LET US UNDERSTAND THE DIFFERENCE BETWEEN WHAT WE **CAN** AND **CANNOT** CONTROL, SO WE MIGHT NOT BE UNNECESSARILY **DISCOURAGED** BY THE **LATTER**.

THE PASSIONS ARE **POWERFUL**, HOWEVER, AND MERE REASON **ALONE** CANNOT HOPE TO STAND AGAINST THEM. ALL THE TIME WE FOOLISHLY "FOLLOW THE **WORSE** COURSE EVEN WHEN WE KNOW THE **BETTER**."

NO, WE NEED TO FIGHT EMOTION WITH ITS **EQUAL**-- REASON'S **OWN** PASSION, WHICH SPINOZA CALLS "THE **INTELLECTUAL** LOVE OF GOD."

UNLIKE **OUR** EMOTIONS, WHICH SO OFTEN ARE UTTERLY **DISPROPORTIONATE** TO THEIR OBJECTS, THE LOVE OF GOD IS WHOLLY "**ACCURATE**" CONTROLLED, AS IT IS, BY **REASON**).

TO KNOW, KNOW, KNOW HIM IS TO LOVE, LOVE, LOVE HIM...

Tiger Beat

...AND I DO...

KNOWING GOD **IS** LOVING GOD, AND **VICE-VERSA**. AND IT IS THE GREATEST LOVE **POSSIBLE**, FOR, BECAUSE WE ARE **PART** OF GOD, OUR LOVE OF GOD IS **ALSO** GOD'S LOVE FOR **HIMSELF**. WHEN WE LOVE **OURSELVES**, WE LOVE THE **UNIVERSE**.

NOK! NOK! NOK!

BIG 'Uns

Kleenx

STAY OUT, MOM! I'M LOVIN' THE UNIVERSE!!

HOWEVER, SPINOZA WRITES, "IT **CANNOT** BE SAID THAT GOD **LOVES** MANKIND, MUCH LESS THAT HE **SHOULD** LOVE THEM BECAUSE **THEY** LOVE HIM, OR **HATE** THEM BECAUSE **THEY** HATE HIM."

>SIGH<... WILL HE EVER **NOTICE** ME?

"HE WHO LOVES GOD **CANNOT** ENDEAVOR THAT GOD SHOULD LOVE HIM IN **RETURN**."

SPINOZA'S GOD DOESN'T **DO** MIRACLES. HE DOESN'T ANSWER YOUR **PRAYERS**.

HE DOESN'T **WATCH** OVER YOU OR YOUR **LOVED ONES** ANY MORE THAN **YOU** SPEND ALL **YOUR** TIME WATCHING OVER DISTINCT PARTS OF YOUR **BODY**.

GOD

NOK! NOK! NOK!

STAY *OUT*, MOM! I'M *WATCHIN'* OVER A DISTINCT PART OF MY *BODY!!*

OH, *STOP.* YOU *KNOW* WHAT WE MEAN...

THAT'S BECAUSE *SPINOZA'S* GOD ISN'T A FATHER, SON, OR *GHOST,* HOLY OR NOT. HE'S NOT NOR HAS HE *EVER* BEEN A *PERSON* LIKE YOU OR ME.

HE IS THE *UNIVERSE.* HE *IS* NATURE. HE IS *YOU.*

NATURE/GOD HAS ALREADY GIVEN YOU *ALL* YOU COULD EVER *NEED,* ALONG WITH THE *REASON* THAT CAN COMPREHEND THIS FACT.

BECAUSE EVERYTHING THAT *IS* IS AS IT *MUST BE,* THERE IS NO *"PURPOSE"* TO LIFE -- WE'RE NOT *"MOVING TOWARDS"* ANY END, AS WE HUMANS CONSTANTLY WONDER AND/OR HOPE.

WE'RE ALREADY *THERE!*

THE *GOOD* NEWS, HOWEVER, IS THAT YOUR *LIFE* CAN'T END, EITHER! "THE HUMAN MIND CANNOT BE *DESTROYED* WITH THE BODY," SPINOZA WRITES. BUT HIS CONCEPTION OF THE *AFTERLIFE,* LIKE HIS CONCEPTION OF *GOD,* IS *WITHOUT PERSONALITY:*

WE MERELY *RETURN* TO THE GOD-SOURCE FROM WHICH WE *SPRANG.* WHEN WE *DIE,* OUR FEELINGS AND MEMORIES DO NOT GO *WITH* US.

BUT IS THAT NOT *FITTING,* AS WHAT *ARE* OUR SELVES OTHER THAN A COLLECTION OF *DESIRES* FOR WHAT WE HAD *ONCE,* AND THINGS THAT WE DON'T HAVE *YET*--AFTER *DEATH,* WHAT *PURPOSE* WOULD YOUR DESIRES SERVE?

ON FEBRUARY 21, 1677, SPINOZA'S PROTESTANT LANDLORD RETURNED HOME FROM CHURCH TO FIND THE GREAT PHILOSOPHER *DEAD.*

THE NEARLY MICROSCOPIC *GLASS DUST* FROM TWENTY-ONE YEARS OF *LENS GRINDING* HAD FLOATED UP, INTO HIS *LUNGS...*

...*DESTROYING* THEM. HE DIED OF ADVANCED *CONSUMPTION* AT *FORTY-FOUR YEARS* OF AGE.

HE PERSISTED IN CLARIFYING *OTHERS'* SIGHT, NO MATTER *WHAT* THE RISK...AND, ULTIMATELY, THAT RISK CAUGHT *UP* TO HIM.

POETIC *TOO,* NO?

GOTTFRIED LEIBNIZ

(1646-1716), co-inventor (along with *ISAAC NEWTON*) of *CALCULUS*, believed he had proven the existence of God through a rather complicated cosmology hinging upon the idea that the universe is made up of an infinite number of points he called *MONADS*, each one of which had the entire universe reflected *in* it, even as it was a distinct PART of the whole...

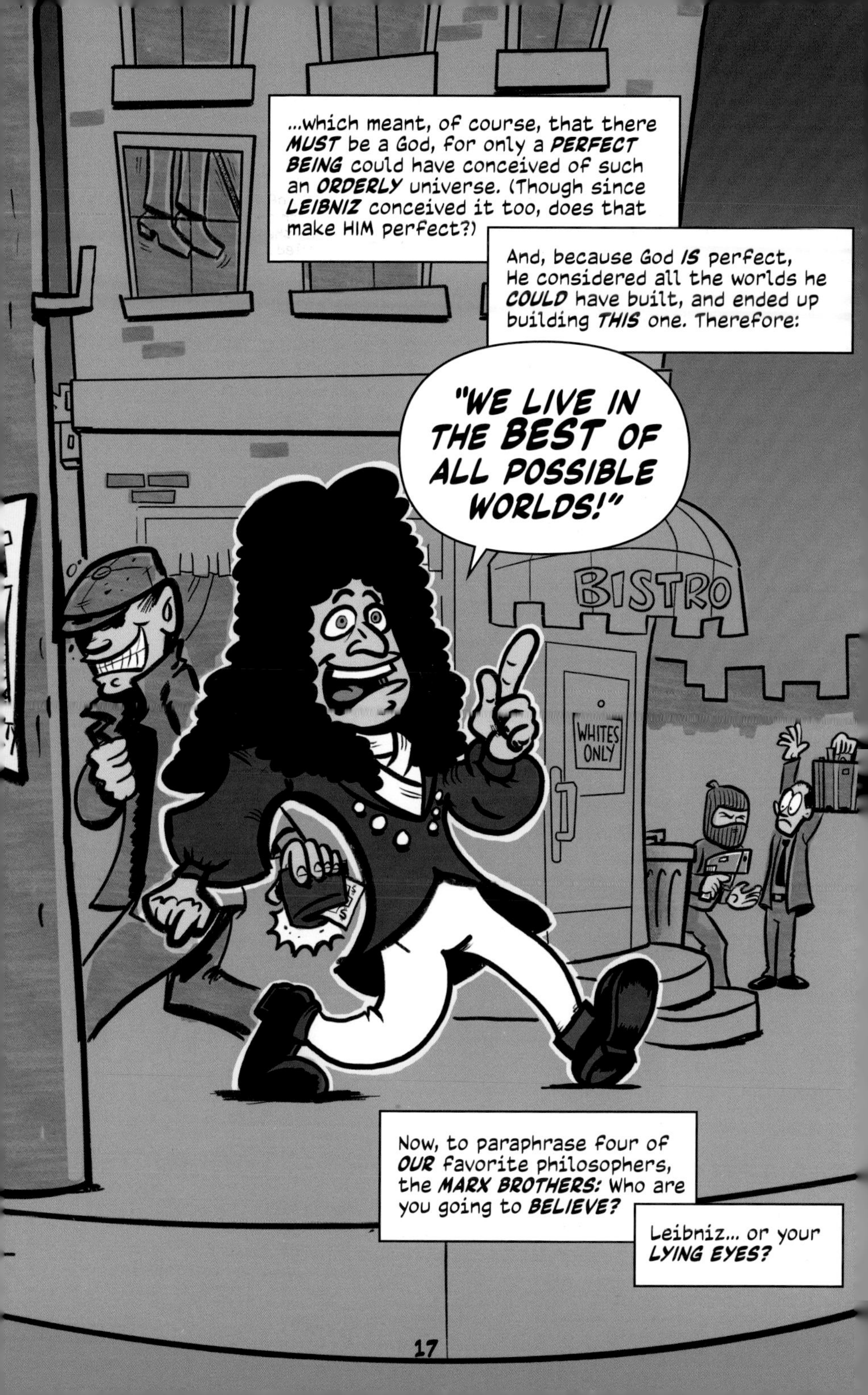

...which meant, of course, that there MUST be a God, for only a PERFECT BEING could have conceived of such an ORDERLY universe. (Though since LEIBNIZ conceived it too, does that make HIM perfect?)
And, because God IS perfect, He considered all the worlds he COULD have built, and ended up building THIS one. Therefore:
"WE LIVE IN THE BEST OF ALL POSSIBLE WORLDS!"
BISTRO
WHITES ONLY
Now, to paraphrase four of OUR favorite philosophers, the MARX BROTHERS: Who are you going to BELIEVE?
Leibniz... or your LYING EYES?

IN 1855, AFTER REPEATED, VEHEMENT ATTACKS ON DENMARK'S *STATE RELIGION*, THE MOST *POPULAR* GUY IN COPENHAGEN WAS MOST DEFINITELY *NOT* ACTION PHILOSOPHER #18:

Søren Kierkegaard

BUT *HE* WAS HAVING THE TIME OF HIS *LIFE!*

WRITTEN (OUT OF *FEAR*) BY *FRED VAN LENTE* DRAWN (THOUGH *TREMBLING*) BY *RYAN DUNLAVEY!*

AH, *HA!* MY ARCH-NEMESIS, THE *DANISH PEOPLE'S CHURCH!*

I'VE GOT YOU *RIGHT* WHERE I *WANT* YOU!

AND I *SWEAR* TO YOU... I *WILL* HAVE THE LAST LAUGH!

THE CHURCH HAD AROUSED THE PHILOSOPHER'S IRE AT THE FUNERAL OF ITS *BISHOP PRIMATE*, J.P. MYNSTER.

FROM *THIS* MAN, WHOSE PRECIOUS MEMORY FILLS OUR HEARTS...

...OUR THOUGHTS ARE LED BACK TO THAT LONG LINE OF SANDHEDSVIDNE*...

* = "WITNESSES TO THE TRUTH" (DANISH)

...WHICH, LIKE A *HOLY CHAIN*, STRETCHES THROUGH TIME FROM THE *APOSTLES* UP TO OUR OWN DAY...

SANDHEDSVIDNE? *SANDHEDSVIDNE?!*

WHAT A *RIP-OFF!!*

THOUGH LARGELY UNKNOWN *OUTSIDE* HIS NATIVE LAND (HE WROTE IN *DANISH*, WHICH DIDN'T HELP), KIERKEGAARD WAS A RESPECTED LITERARY FIGURE *WITHIN* DENMARK.

OHHHHHH...

...*NOW* I GET IT!

HE HAD *COINED* THE TERM "SANDHEDSVIDNE" IN *CHRISTIAN DISCOURSES* (1848) TO DESCRIBE *MARTYRS* WHO CAME INTO A FULL UNDER-STANDING OF LIFE THROUGH *SUFFERING!*

IN EARLIER WORKS, KIERKEGAARD HAD DESCRIBED THE *RELIGIOUS* STAGE OF LIFE AS THE *CULMINATION* OF THE *THREE* STAGES OF DEVELOPMENT OF HUMAN *SELF-CONSCIOUSNESS!*

HE PERSONIFIED THESE STAGES IN THE CHARACTERS OF *DON JUAN*, SOCRATES, AND THE *WANDERING JEW!*

HELLO? *TRIPLE-A*? THIS IS *MYRON EPSTEIN*...

DON JUAN REPRESENTS THE **AESTHETIC** STAGE OF LIFE, IN WHICH A PERSON IS RULED BY HIS IMPULSES AND **EMOTIONS**. HE PLACES NO **LIMITATIONS** ON HIS EXISTENCE SAVE **TASTE**; HE CARES NOT FOR THE **QUALITY** OF HIS EXPERIENCES... ONLY FOR THEIR **VARIETY** AND **NUMBER**!

THE **RATIONAL** MAN, HOWEVER, PERCEIVES THERE IS A **HIGHER** FACULTY THAN THE SENSES, AND HE IS **DRAWN** TO IT.

HE ENTERS THE **ETHICAL** STAGE, EXEMPLIFIED BY **SOCRATES**. HE REFLECTS ON AND APPLIES **UNIVERSAL MORALITY** TO HIS LIFE...

...LIKE THE **BACHELOR** WHO VOLUNTEERS TO CONSTRICT HIS **SEXUAL IMPULSES** BY THE **ETHICAL CONTRACT** OF **MARRIAGE**!

YET THE ETHICAL MAN DISCOVERS THAT OBEYING MORAL LAW BRINGS **SUFFERING**, SO HE HAS TO MAKE A **"LEAP OF FAITH"** (ANOTHER KIERKEGAARD-COINED TERM)...

...INTO THE **IRRATIONALITY** OF RELIGIOUS BELIEF, SYMBOLIZED BY THE PARADOX OF **CHRIST**: THE ETERNAL (*GOD*) ENSCRIBED BY THE MORTAL (*JESUS*)!

HEY, IF YOU DIDN'T STRUGGLE WITH **DOUBT**, IT WOULDN'T BE **FAITH**, NOW WOULD IT?

YOU CAN'T HAVE **FAITH** IN THINGS YOU KNOW FOR A **FACT** EXIST!

I'M SOLD!

RATIONALITY

20

THE PROBLEM WITH THE *ETHICAL* MAN IS THAT HE IS OBSESSED WITH THE *ABSTRACT*. "PHILOSOPHICAL PROBLEMS" AMOUNT TO LITTLE MORE THAN HYPOTHETICAL *DETOURS* AROUND LIFE'S NECESSARY *CHOICES*.

RATIONALLY, THERE MAY BE REASONS FOR *OR* AGAINST ANY GIVEN DECISION. BUT HUMANS, IN ORDER TO LIVE *IN* THE WORLD, *MUST* SET RATIONALITY ASIDE AND *CHOOSE ONE*.

BEING

WHERE'S THE @#$! OFF-RAMP?!

"THE PARADOX OF FAITH IS *THIS*," KIERKEGAARD WRITES IN *FEAR & TREMBLING* (1843):

"THAT THE INDIVIDUAL IS *HIGHER* THAN THE UNIVERSAL, THAT THE INDIVIDUAL DETERMINES HIS *RELATION* TO THE UNIVERSAL BY HIS RELATION TO THE *ABSOLUTE*."

Individual   Universal   Absolute

THE RELIGIOUS MAN DETERMINES THIS RELATION BY WHAT KIERKEGAARD CALLS "*INFINITE RESIGNATION*".

AS IN THE CASE OF A KNIGHT WHO SO LOVES A FAIR *PRINCESS*...

...THAT HE *GIVES HER UP* TO ANOTHER!

BY THIS, "HE KEEPS THIS LOVE *YOUNG*, AND ALONG WITH *HIM* IT INCREASES IN YEARS AND IN *BEAUTY*."

21

"HE HAS NO NEED OF THOSE EROTIC TINGLINGS IN THE NERVES AT THE SIGHT OF HIS BELOVED *ETC.*, NOR DOES HE NEED TO BE CONSTANTLY TAKING LEAVE OF HER IN A *FINITE* SENSE..."

"...BECAUSE HE RECOLLECTS HER IN AN *ETERNAL* SENSE!"

"TO BECOME A CHRISTIAN ACCORDING TO THE NEW TESTAMENT IS TO BECOME *'SPIRIT.'*"

"TO BECOME SPIRIT ACCORDING TO THE NEW TESTAMENT IS TO *DIE OFF* FROM THE WORLD."

"FOR DYING IS FAIRLY *BRIEF* SUFFERING, WHEREAS DYING OFF LASTS THE *WHOLE* OF ONE'S LIFE!"

KIERKEGAARD SET ABOUT "DYING OFF FROM THE WORLD" NOT LONG AFTER RECEIVING HIS DOCTORATE IN *THEOLOGY* IN 1841.

THAT SAME YEAR HE INEXPLICABLY BROKE OFF HIS ENGAGEMENT TO *REGINE OLSEN*, THE LOVE OF HIS LIFE!

HE *REVELED* IN HIS ROLE AS A SELF-PROCLAIMED *OUTSIDER*, AN *"EXCEPTION"*...

...READING, WRITING, AND THINKING LARGELY IN *SOLITUDE* IN HIS COPENHAGEN APARTMENT, ALL THE WHILE SUPPORTING HIMSELF ON A SIZEABLE *INHERITANCE*.

AFTER FLIRTING FOR A TIME WITH HEGELIAN *IDEALISM*, KIERKEGAARD FOUND AT LAST IN *CHRISTIANITY* THAT FOR WHICH HE HAD BEEN STRIVING FOR ALL HIS LIFE:

NOW HIRING: IDEAS

"THE THING IS TO FIND A *TRUTH* WHICH IS *TRUE FOR ME*, TO FIND THE IDEA FOR WHICH I CAN LIVE AND *DIE*."

KIERKEGAARD'S WORKS WERE *REDISCOVERED* BY ACADEMIA IN THE 1950'S, WHEN *EXISTENTIALISM* WAS ALL THE RAGE. BECAUSE HE'S *MORBID* AND TALKS ABOUT *CHOICES* A LOT, MANY REGARD KIERKEGAARD AS "THE *FATHER* OF EXISTENTIALISM"...

ARE *YOU* MY *DADDY?*

...BUT THAT SEEMS TOUGH TO RECONCILE WITH HIS FUNDAMENTALLY *RELIGIOUS* THINKING:

"A MAN IS BORN IN SIN, ENTERS THIS WORLD BY MEANS OF A *CRIME*. THE *PUNISHMENT*-- AND, AS ALWAYS, THE PUNISHMENT FITS THE *SIN*--"

LIFE

"--THE PUNISHMENT IS TO *EXIST.*"

BUT: "*THIS* IS WHAT CHRISTIANITY IS FOR--WHICH STRAIGHTAWAY *BARS* THE WAY TO *PROCREATION*. THIS MEANS:"

"*STOP!* I HAVE PUT UP *LONG ENOUGH* WITH THIS WORLD-HISTORICAL PROCESS."

"*CERTAINLY* I WILL HAVE *PITY*, BUT I DO NOT WANT *ANY MORE* OF THE CONSEQUENCES OF THAT *FALSE STEP.*"

"AND THAT IS WHY CHRISTIANITY UPHOLDS *CELIBACY*. BY *THIS* THE CHRISTIAN GIVES CHARACTERISTIC EXPRESSION TO HIS RELATIONSHIP TO THE *WORLD*...WHICH IS AN *OBLIGATION* TO STOP IT!"

WE'RE THE *LAST MAN* AND THE *LAST WOMAN* ON EARTH, AND NEVER *ONCE* DID WE MAKE *WHOOPIE!*

WHEN WE *DIE*, HUMANITY ENDS... AND GOD *WINS!*

RIP

"AS A CONSEQUENCE OF CHRISTIANITY, TO *LOVE GOD* MEANS TO *HATE THE WORLD!*"

HAD *ENOUGH?*

KIERKEGAARD SPENT MUCH OF HIS LITERARY CAREER EXTOLLING SUCH EXTREME *SACRIFICE* AS MANDATORY FOR A TRULY *CHRISTIAN LIFE*. SO WHEN AT BISHOP MYNSTER'S FUNERAL HE *HEARD*--

...THAT LONG LINE OF *SANDHEDSVIDNE*...

--HE *BLEW HIS STACK!*

"WITNESS TO THE TRUTH" MY *FOOT!*

MYNSTER WOULDN'T RECOGNIZE TRUTH IF IT SLITHERED OUT OF HIS GOLD-PLATED *CASSOCK* AND BIT HIM ON THE *NOSE!*

MOST *NATIONAL* CHURCHES ARE *POLITICAL* ENTITIES AS MUCH AS THEY ARE *RELIGIOUS* ONES--IN *DENMARK*, IN FACT, THE CHURCH HAD A *CABINET SEAT!*

I DO SO *LOVE* THE *WORLD!* HAW!

THE BISHOP WAS THE PERSONAL PASTOR TO THE COUNTRY'S *RICH* AND *POWERFUL*--NOT TO MENTION BEING ONE OF BOTH *HIMSELF!*

FOR KIERKEGAARD, "PRECISELY IN THE SENSE THAT A CHILD PLAYS *SOLDIER* IT IS *PLAYING* AT CHRISTIANITY TO TAKE AWAY THE *DANGER* (CHRISTIANLY, *'WITNESS'* AND *'DANGER'* CORRESPOND), AND IN ITS PLACE TO INTRODUCE *POWER* ... WORLDLY GOODS, ADVANTAGES, LUXURIOUS ENJOYMENT OF THE MOST EXQUISITE *REFINEMENTS*."

BLESS YOU, MOMMY!

AW, ISN'T THAT *CUTE?*

HE WAS ESPECIALLY *GALLED* THAT A WORD OF HIS OWN COINAGE HAD BEEN APPLIED TO A MAN WHOM HE FELT REPRESENTED THE *EXACT OPPOSITE* OF EVERYTHING GOOD AND SPECIAL IN THE CHRISTIAN FAITH!

ALRIGHT, DANISH PEOPLE'S CHURCH...

...*THIS TIME*, IT'S *PERSONAL!*

BETWEEN MAY AND SEPTEMBER 1855 HE BANKROLLED TEN ISSUES OF ØIEBLIKKET ("THE INSTANT"), HIS SELF-PUBLISHED ASSAULT ON THE DANISH CHURCH!

CENTRAL TO HIS OBJECTIONS WAS THAT CHRISTIANITY WAS A "PRIVATE" RELIGION THAT BECAME BANKRUPTED ONCE INCORPORATED INTO THE ESTABLISHMENT.

CHRISTIAN CLONING MACHINE

HAAAALP! ~GLUB!~

IF PEOPLE COULD BE BORN CHRISTIANS, IT RENDERED THE INDIVIDUAL CHOICE OF "INFINITE RESIGNATION" NOT JUST MEANINGLESS, BUT IMPOSSIBLE!

THOUGH THE INSTANT CAUSED A STIR AT FIRST, MOST DANES GREW TO SEE KIERKEGAARD'S POLEMICS AS REPETITIVE, PETTY BITCHING.

SHOULD WE EXCOMMUNICATE THE NUT?

WHY BOTHER? IT'S NOT LIKE ANYONE IS LISTENING.

THOUGH HE EXHAUSTED HIS SAVINGS PRODUCING THE INSTANT, REGINE OLSEN REPORTED SHE HAD NEVER SEEN KIERKEGAARD SO HAPPY:

"I FEEL MYSELF REALLY IN MY ELEMENT ONLY WHEN I AM SURROUNDED BY HUMAN MEDIOCRITY AND PALTRINESS!"

HE FELL DEATHLY ILL AT THE BEGINNING OF OCTOBER 1855, AND HAD TO BE HOSPITALIZED. AS HIS CONDITION WORSENED, HE REFUSED COMMUNION UNLESS A LAYMAN, NOT A PRIEST, PERFORMED IT.

"THE CLERGY ARE STATE FUNCTIONARIES, AND FUNCTIONARIES HAVE NOTHING TO DO WITH CHRISTIANITY!"

HE DIED AT 9 AT NIGHT ON NOVEMBER 11.

AT THE FUNERAL, KIERKEGAARD'S ONLY LIVING SIBLING, *PETER*, HIMSELF A *PRIEST*, INSISTED THAT THE D.P.C.'S *ARCHDEACON TRYDE* DELIVER THE COMMITTAL:

MAY GOD HAVE *MERCY* ON THIS *BEWILDERED, PERPLEXED SOUL...*

KIERKEGAARD'S NEPHEW *HENRIK* GREW ANGRIER AND ANGRIER THROUGHOUT THE SERVICE, UNTIL *FINALLY*:

I MUST *PROTEST* THE WAY THE CHURCH HAS TREATED MY UNCLE TODAY!

HE DECLARED *OFTEN* IN HIS WRITINGS THAT HE WAS *NOT A CHRISTIAN!*

THAT'S A *LIE!*

YOU *KNOW* WHAT I MEAN -- THE *"AUTOMATIC"* KIND OF CHRISTIAN HE *DESPISED!*

YET THE CHURCH HAS *SEIZED* HIS BODY--*FORCED* HIM TO BE COMMITTED TO *ETERNITY* AS SUCH A CHRISTIAN!

WOULD A *RABBI* FORCE A CONVERTED JEW TO BE BURIED A JEW? WOULD A *TURK* (MUSLIM)?

NO, ONLY *CHRISTIANS* DO THIS! WHAT *REVELATIONS* SAYS IS *TRUE*--

--THE *STATE CHURCH* IS A *WHORE* SCREWED BY ALL THE *TYRANTS* OF THE *EARTH!*

YOU ARE *RAPING* MY UNCLE'S *MEMORY!*

STOP THIS *THIEF!* HE IS *DESECRATING* HOLY PLACES!

AND SO SOREN KIERKEGAARD HAD THE MOST *APPROPRIATE* FUNERAL IN HUMAN HISTORY!

I *TOLD* YOU I'D HAVE THE *LAST LAUGH!*

-:HEH, HEH!:-

George Berkeley

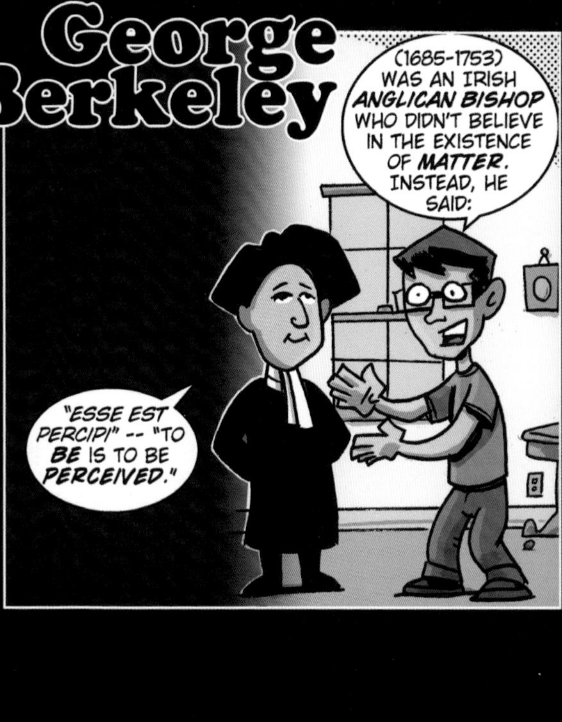
(1685-1753) WAS AN IRISH ANGLICAN BISHOP WHO DIDN'T BELIEVE IN THE EXISTENCE OF MATTER. INSTEAD, HE SAID:
"ESSE EST PERCIPI" -- "TO BE IS TO BE PERCEIVED."

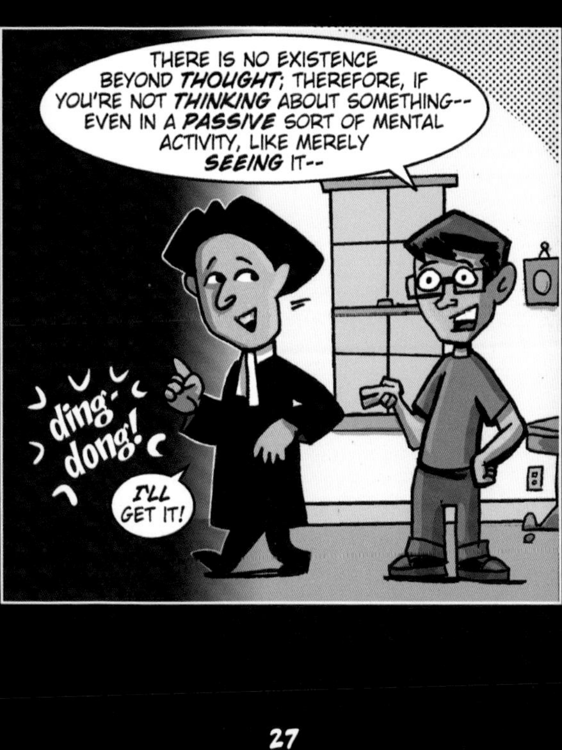
THERE IS NO EXISTENCE BEYOND THOUGHT; THEREFORE, IF YOU'RE NOT THINKING ABOUT SOMETHING-- EVEN IN A PASSIVE SORT OF MENTAL ACTIVITY, LIKE MERELY SEEING IT--
ding-dong!
I'LL GET IT!

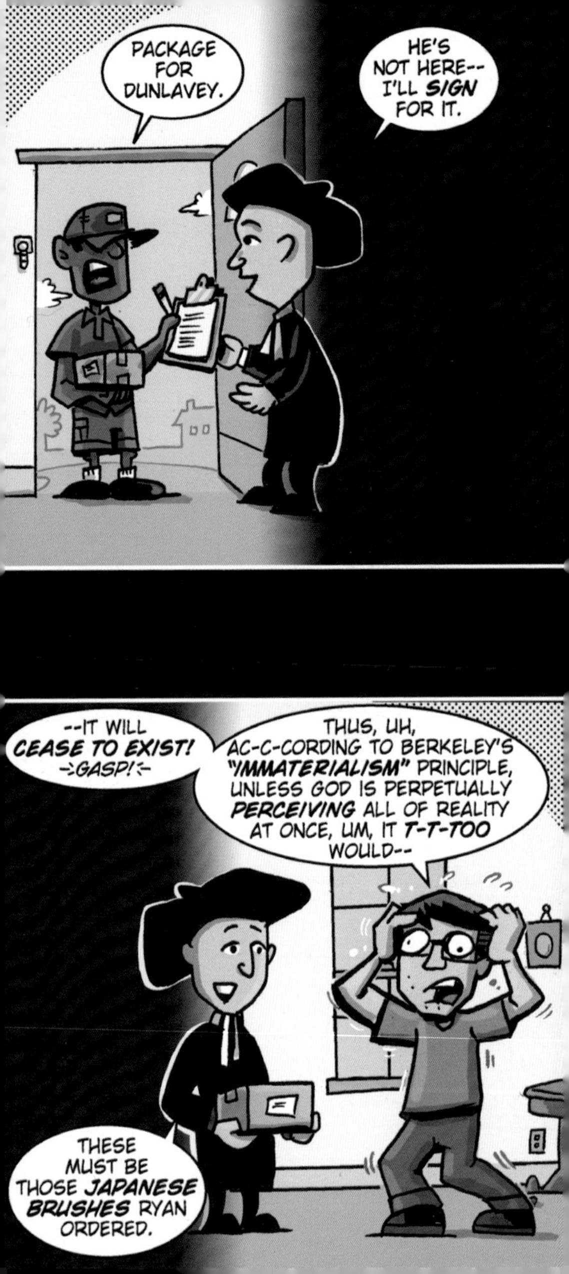
PACKAGE FOR DUNLAVEY.
HE'S NOT HERE-- I'LL SIGN FOR IT.
THUS, UH, AC-C-CORDING TO BERKELEY'S "IMMATERIALISM" PRINCIPLE, UNLESS GOD IS PERPETUALLY PERCEIVING ALL OF REALITY AT ONCE, UM, IT T-T-TOO WOULD--
--IT WILL CEASE TO EXIST! GASP!
THESE MUST BE THOSE JAPANESE BRUSHES RYAN ORDERED.

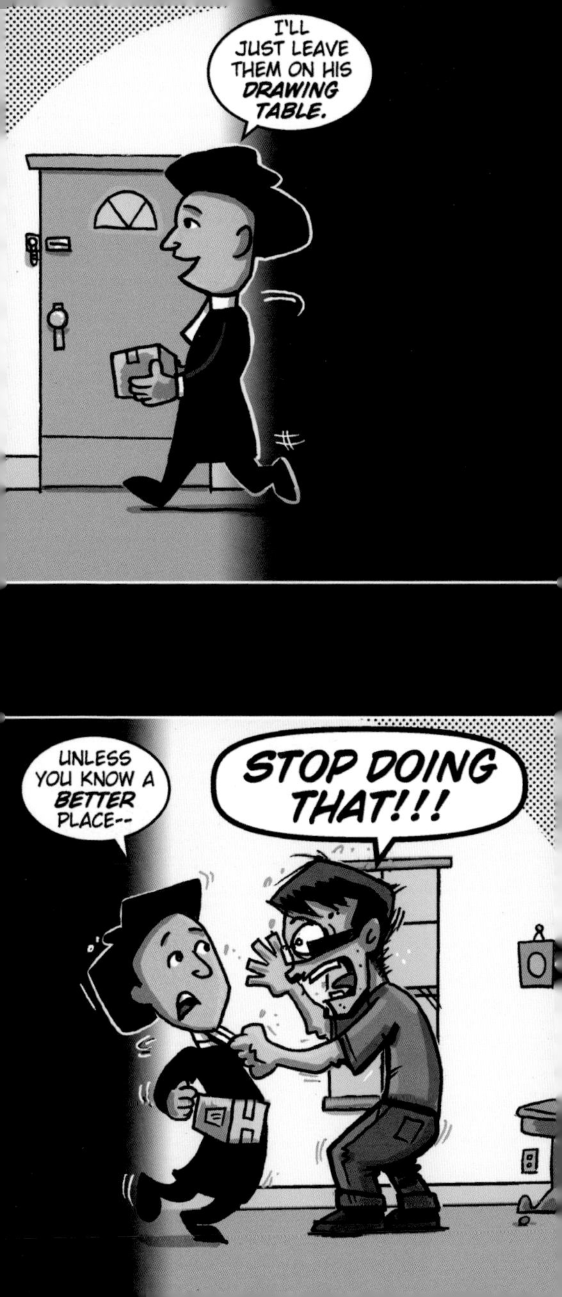
I'LL JUST LEAVE THEM ON HIS *DRAWING TABLE.*
UNLESS YOU KNOW A *BETTER* PLACE--
STOP DOING THAT!!!

PLATO

ATLANTIS

wrote in his *Critias* about the sinking of

TEMPEST

AQUALAD

home to

whom D.C. Comics renamed

KNOWLEDGE IS POWER.*

*"NAM ET IPSA SCIENTIA POTESTAS EST" -MEDITATIONES SACRAE (1597)

title of the last play by

SHAKESPEARE

who some scholars believe didn't write anything--that all the plays attributed to him were actually written by

STUFFING A CHICKEN WITH SNOW

which in 1626 is what killed

RENE DESCARTES

which can also be caught by

PNEUMONIA

died in 1650 by trudging to and from the swedish court in mid-winter and caught

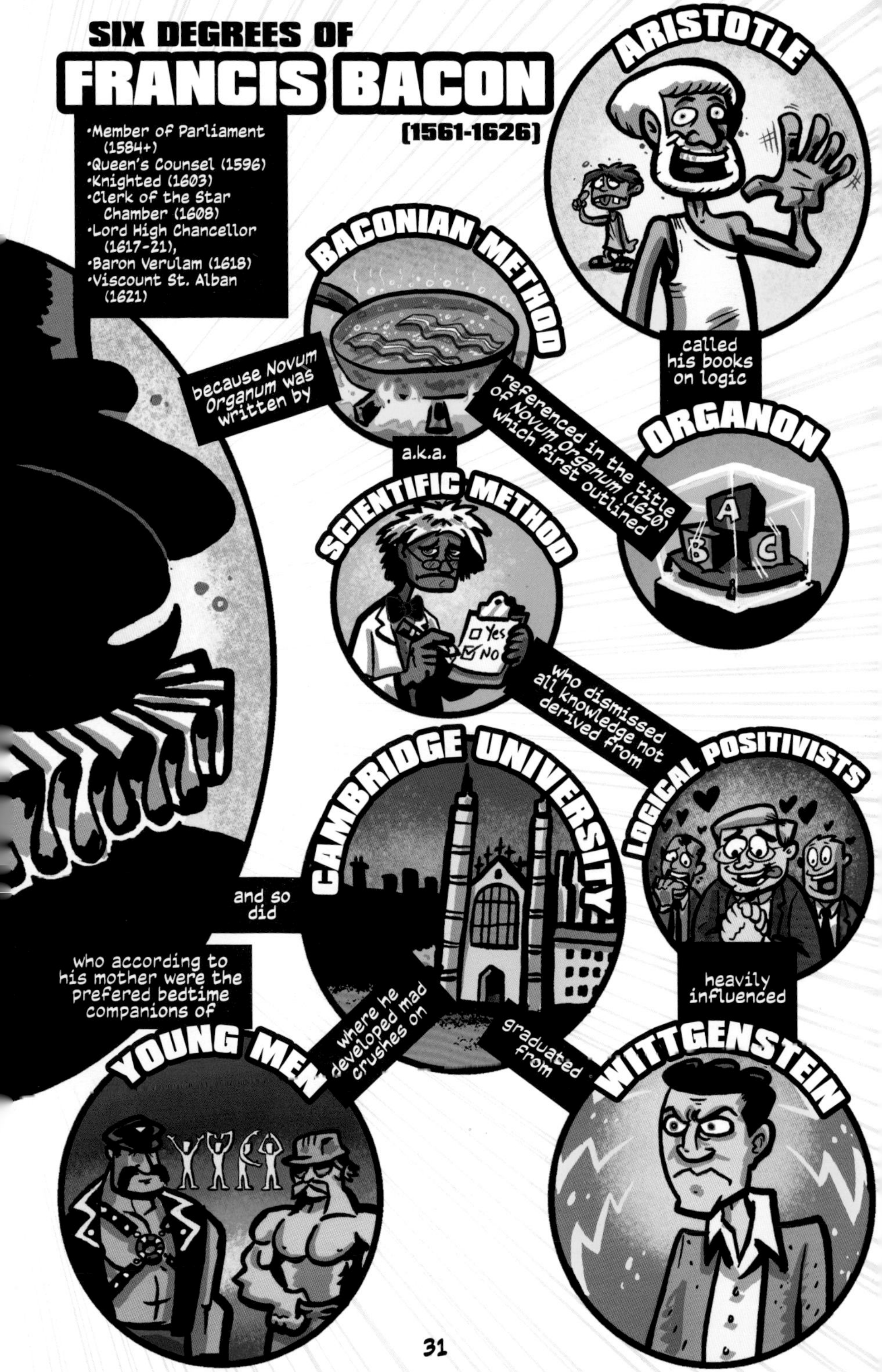
SIX DEGREES OF
FRANCIS BACON
(1561-1626)
•Member of Parliament (1584+)
•Queen's Counsel (1596)
•Knighted (1603)
•Clerk of the Star Chamber (1608)
•Lord High Chancellor (1617-21),
•Baron Verulam (1618)
•Viscount St. Alban (1621)
ARISTOTLE
called his books on logic
ORGANON
referenced in the title of Novum Organum (1620) which first outlined
BACONIAN METHOD
because Novum Organum was written by
a.k.a.
SCIENTIFIC METHOD
Yes
No
who dismissed all knowledge not derived from
LOGICAL POSITIVISTS
heavily influenced
WITTGENSTEIN
graduated from
CAMBRIDGE UNIVERSITY
and so did
where he developed mad crushes on
YOUNG MEN
who according to his mother were the prefered bedtime companions of

DAVID HUME

IF IT'S NOT **EMPIRRRICAL**, IT'S **CRRRAP!**

THE BRANCH OF PHILOSOPHY KNOWN AS **EMPIRICISM** HAS BEEN PRACTICED PRIMARILY IN THE **BRITISH ISLES.**

"IF WE TAKE IN OUR HAND ANY VOLUME OF DIVINITY OR SCHOOL OF META-PHYSICS... LET US ASK:"

"DOES IT CONTAIN ANY **ABSTRACT REASONING** CONCERNING **QUANTITY** OR **NUMBER?**"

ENGLISHMAN **JOHN LOCKE'S** (1632-1704) **ESSAY CONCERNING HUMAN UNDERSTANDING** (1690) INSPIRED IT...

AAAAAAH!

NO? IT'S **CRRRAP!**

FWOOSH!!!

...FOR, LOCKE ASSERTS, CONTRARY TO THE INTELLECTUAL **OPTIMISM** OF A BACON OR DESCARTES, THE SCOPE OF OUR KNOWLEDGE IS LIMITED BY **EXPERIENCE.**

"DOES IT CONTAIN ANY **EXPERIMENTAL** REASONING CONCERNING MATTER OF FACT AND **EXISTENCE?**"

THERE IS A **WALL** BEYOND WHICH HUMAN REASON IS **INCAPABLE** OF UNDERSTANDING!

NO? CRRAP!!

IF NOT, "COMMIT IT TO THE **FLAMES:** FOR IT CONTAINS NOTHING BUT SOPHISTRY AND **ILLUSION!**"*

FWOOSH!!!

*: D.H., **ENQUIRY CONCERNING HUMAN UNDER-STANDING** (1748)

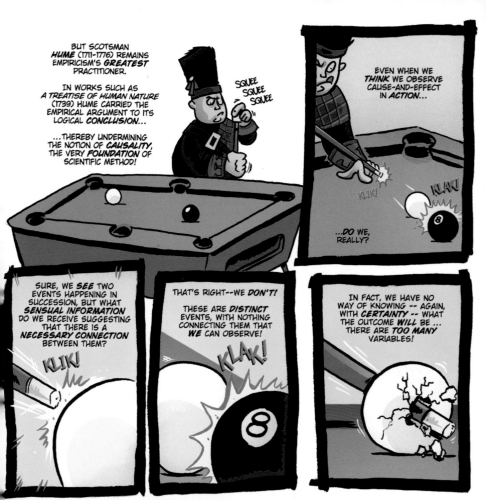

BUT SCOTSMAN *HUME* (1711-1776) REMAINS EMPIRICISM'S *GREATEST* PRACTITIONER.

IN WORKS SUCH AS *A TREATISE OF HUMAN NATURE* (1739) HUME CARRIED THE EMPIRICAL ARGUMENT TO ITS LOGICAL *CONCLUSION*...

...THEREBY UNDERMINING THE NOTION OF *CAUSALITY*, THE VERY *FOUNDATION* OF SCIENTIFIC METHOD!

SQUEE SQUEE SQUEE

EVEN WHEN WE *THINK* WE OBSERVE CAUSE-AND-EFFECT IN *ACTION*...

KLIK!

KLAK!

8

...DO WE, REALLY?

SURE, WE *SEE* TWO EVENTS HAPPENING IN SUCCESSION, BUT WHAT *SENSUAL INFORMATION* DO WE RECEIVE SUGGESTING THAT THERE IS A *NECESSARY CONNECTION* BETWEEN THEM?

KLIK!

THAT'S RIGHT--WE *DON'T!*

THESE ARE *DISTINCT* EVENTS, WITH NOTHING CONNECTING THEM THAT *WE* CAN OBSERVE!

KLAK!

8

IN FACT, WE HAVE NO WAY OF KNOWING -- AGAIN, WITH *CERTAINTY* -- WHAT THE OUTCOME *WILL* BE ... THERE ARE *TOO MANY* VARIABLES!

HUME CALLED THESE PROBLEMS OF *INDUCTION*-- WHEN EXPERIENCE *SUPPORTS* A CONCLUSION WITHOUT *ENSURING* IT.

FOR INSTANCE, WE HAVE NO *IRONCLAD EMPIRICAL DATA* THAT GUARANTEES THAT THE SUN WILL *RISE* TOMORROW!

BY THE *SAME* LOGIC, HUME SAID YOUR SENSE OF PERSONAL IDENTITY OR *SELF* IS *ALSO* ILLUSORY. TAKE YOURSELF FROM WHAT YOU'RE PROBABLY THINKING *THIS* MOMENT *RIGHT NOW*:

GOSH, FRED AND RYAN ARE SO FUNNY *AND* SMART! I BET THEY'RE *HOT* TOO ... I WISH I COULD SLEEP WITH *BOTH* OF THEM!

ACTION PHILOSOPHERS

SEPARATELY, I MEAN.

"WHEN I ENTER MOST *INTIMATELY* INTO WHAT I CALL *MYSELF*," HUME WRITES, "I ALWAYS STUMBLE ON SOME PARTICULAR *PERCEPTION* OR OTHER, OF HEAT OR COLD, LOVE OR HATRED, PAIN OR PLEASURE. I NEVER CAN CATCH *MYSELF* AT ANY TIME *WITHOUT* A PERCEPTION AND NEVER CAN OBSERVE ANYTHING *BUT* THE PERCEPTION."

SEPARATELY, I MEAN.

CLASS OF '02 RULES!! WHOOOOO!!

WAIT HERE, HONEY--I'LL GET THE BACTINE!

WAAAAAA!!

IN OTHER WORDS, OUR ALLEGED *IDENTITIES* ARE NOTHING MORE THAN THE SUM OF THE *PERCEPTIONS* WE'VE ACCUMULATED -- IT IS ONLY THAT "HABIT OF *ASSOCIATION*" THAT CREATES CAUSE-AND-EFFECT THAT LEADS US TO BELIEVE WE HAVE ONE *CONTINUOUS SELF* -- THAT WE ARE THE *SAME PERSON* IN *EACH* OF THE MOMENTS OF OUR LIVES!

"LET US CHASE OUR IMAGINATION TO THE *HEAVENS*, OR THE UTMOST LIMITS OF THE *UNIVERSE*," HUME SAYS...

"WE NEVER ADVANCE A STEP *BEYOND* OURSELVES..."

"...NOR CAN WE CONCEIVE ANY *KIND* OF EXISTENCE..."

"...BUT THOSE *PERCEPTIONS* WHICH HAVE APPEARED IN THAT *NARROW* COMPASS."

HELP!

"*THIS* IS THE UNIVERSE OF THE *IMAGINATION*, NOR HAVE WE *ANY* IDEA BUT WHAT IS *THERE* PRODUCED."

IDEA

BUT THIS INABILITY FOR US TO KNOW ANYTHING OUTSIDE *OURSELVES* SHOULDN'T MAKE YOU THINK HUME ADVOCATES *MORAL RELATIVISM.*

25¢

PLEASE HELP GOD BLESS

NO, FOR HUME, *MORALITY* HAS NOTHING TO DO WITH *REASON* -- RATHER, IT IS THE FACULTY OF *SYMPATHY* THAT GUIDES THE *RIGHT-NESS* OF OUR ACTIONS!

"IT IS NEEDLESS TO PUSH OUR RESEARCHES SO FAR AS TO ASK, *WHY* WE HAVE HUMANITY OR A FELLOW-FEELING WITH OTHERS," HUME WROTE. "IT IS SUFFICIENT, THAT THIS IS *EXPERIENCED* TO BE A *PRINCIPLE* OF HUMAN NATURE."

PLEASE HELP GOD BLESS

SYMPATHY MAKES US FEEL *GOOD* WHEN WE DO GOOD THINGS--BAD OR *GUILTY* WHEN WE DO *BAD* THINGS!

INDEED, HUME CONCLUDES, "REASON IS AND *OUGHT* TO BE THE SLAVE OF THE *PASSIONS.*" PERHAPS THIS IS WHY HUME'S *NICKNAME* AMONG HIS CONTEMPORARIES WAS *LE BON DAVID.*

WALK

"IN ALL MY LIFE, DID I NEVER MEET WITH A BEING OF A MORE *PLACID* AND *GENTLE* NATURE," A CRITIC OF THE DAY WROTE, "AND IT IS THIS *AMIABLE* TURN OF HIS CHARACTER THAT HAS GIVEN MORE CONSEQUENCE AND *FORCE* TO HIS SKEPTICISM, THAN ALL THE ARGUMENTS OF HIS *SOPHISTRY.*"

WE ARE RESCUED FROM ANY *PESSIMISM* ABOUT REASON'S LIMITS BY A KIND OF BENIGN *ATTENTION DEFICIT DISORDER:*

"I *DINE,* I PLAY A GAME OF *BACKGAMMON,* I CONVERSE AND AM MERRY WITH MY *FRIENDS...*"

"...AND WHEN AFTER THREE OR FOUR HOURS' AMUSEMENT I WOULD RETURN TO THESE SPECULATIONS..."

"...THEY APPEAR SO COLD, SO STRAINED, AND *RIDICULOUS* THAT I CANNOT FIND IT IN MY HEART TO ENTER INTO THEM ANY *FURTHER!*"

IN OTHER WORDS, ANY CONTEMPLATION OF REASON'S *LIMITS* IS JUST ONE MORE *PERCEPTION* TO BE ADDED TO THE *SUM* OF YOUR LIFE!

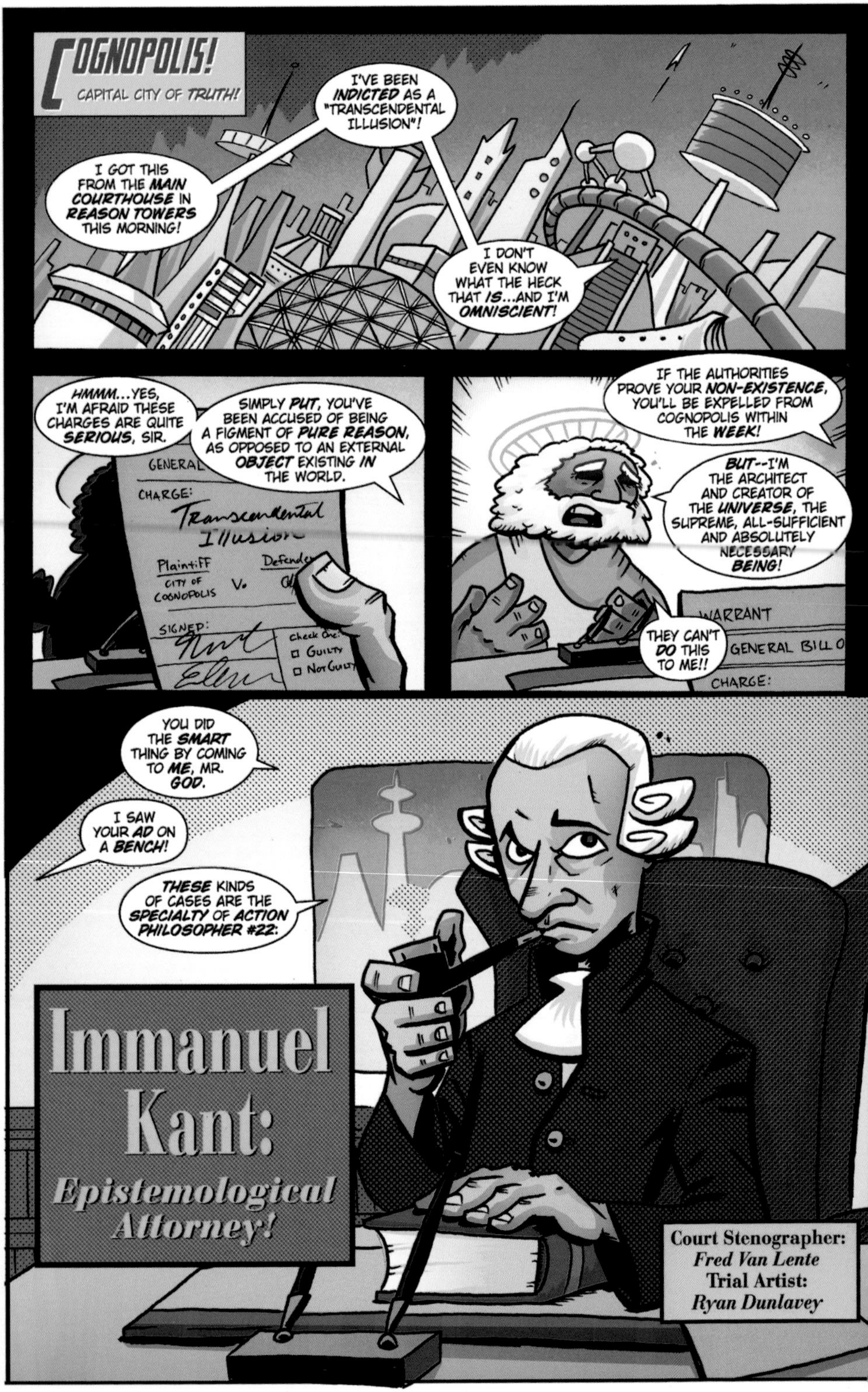
COGNOPOLIS!
CAPITAL CITY OF TRUTH!
I GOT THIS FROM THE MAIN COURTHOUSE IN REASON TOWERS THIS MORNING!
I'VE BEEN INDICTED AS A "TRANSCENDENTAL ILLUSION"!
I DON'T EVEN KNOW WHAT THE HECK THAT IS...AND I'M OMNISCIENT!
HMMM...YES, I'M AFRAID THESE CHARGES ARE QUITE SERIOUS, SIR.
SIMPLY PUT, YOU'VE BEEN ACCUSED OF BEING A FIGMENT OF PURE REASON, AS OPPOSED TO AN EXTERNAL OBJECT EXISTING IN THE WORLD.
GENERAL
CHARGE:
Transcendental Illusion
Plaintiff
CITY OF COGNOPOLIS
V.
SIGNED:
Check One:
Guilty
Not Guilty
IF THE AUTHORITIES PROVE YOUR NON-EXISTENCE, YOU'LL BE EXPELLED FROM COGNOPOLIS WITHIN THE WEEK!
BUT--I'M THE ARCHITECT AND CREATOR OF THE UNIVERSE, THE SUPREME, ALL-SUFFICIENT AND ABSOLUTELY NECESSARY BEING!
THEY CAN'T DO THIS TO ME!!
WARRANT
GENERAL BILL O
CHARGE:
YOU DID THE SMART THING BY COMING TO ME, MR. GOD.
I SAW YOUR AD ON A BENCH!
THESE KINDS OF CASES ARE THE SPECIALTY OF ACTION PHILOSOPHER #22:
Immanuel Kant: Epistemological Attorney!
Court Stenographer: Fred Van Lente
Trial Artist: Ryan Dunlavey

dum-DUM!

SUPREME COURT
TRIAL PART 43
TUESDAY, MARCH 5

YOUR *NAME*, SIR?

AUDIE. AUDIE *BULL*.

AND YOUR *OCCUPATION*?

"I'M THE GRAVEYARD SHIFT *SUPERVISOR* AT THE HEARING PLANT DOWN IN *SENSUOUS FLATS*."

"I *LIKE* THE WORK. THE BIG I TENDS TO BE *ASLEEP* WHEN I'M THERE, SO THE SOUNDS WE RECEIVE ARE USUALLY PRETTY *MELLOW*."

tick-tock tick-tock

zZZz *meow.*

YOU ARE NO DOUBT FAMILIAR WITH THE SO-CALLED *"ONTOLOGICAL"* PROOF OF THE DEFENDANT'S EXISTENCE. IN YOUR PROFESSIONAL *JUDGMENT*--

WHOA! *HEY!* HOLD UP THERE! *UNION RULES* SAY WE DON'T GOT TO DO NO *JUDGMENTS* IN SENSUOUS FLATS!

WE'RE JUST *WORKIN' STIFFS!* WE HAUL RAW DATA TO THEM EGGHEADS IN *UNDERSTANDING HEIGHTS* FOR ALL THAT FANCY-SCHAMNCY THINKIN' AND REASONIN'!

OF COURSE, MY *APOLOGIES*, MR. BULL. I SHALL *REPHRASE*:

SOME SAY THAT WE COULD NOT CONCEIVE OF THE *IDEA* OF THE DEFENDANT WITHOUT AN *OBJECT* CORRESPONDING TO THAT IDEA ACTUALLY *EXISTING*.

"EXCEPT WHAT WE KNOW OF *EXISTENCE* COMES ONLY *A POSTERIORI* (*AFTER* EMPIRICAL EXPERIENCE)...

...*NOT* AS PURE CONCEPTIONS OF THE MIND *BEFORE* (*A PRIORI*) EXPERIENCE THAT ARE *INDEPENDENT* OF SENSUOUS IMPRESSIONS!"

a posteriori

a posteriori

a priori

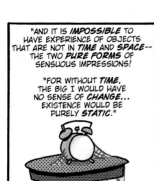

"AND IT IS *IMPOSSIBLE* TO HAVE EXPERIENCE OF OBJECTS THAT ARE NOT IN *TIME* AND *SPACE*-- THE TWO *PURE FORMS* OF SENSUOUS IMPRESSIONS!"

"FOR WITHOUT *TIME*, THE BIG I WOULD HAVE NO SENSE OF *CHANGE*... EXISTENCE WOULD BE PURELY *STATIC*."

"AND WITHOUT *SPACE*, WE WOULD HAVE NO SENSE OF AN *EXTERNAL WORLD* --

THE BIG I WOULD HAVE NO SENSE OF ANYTHING EXISTING *OUTSIDE HIMSELF!*"

MY BEING... *UGH!*...IS A LITTLE... *CONSTIPATED!*

"WE OF COGNOPOLIS TERM THESE *A POSTERIORI* IMPRESSIONS FROM A SPACE/TIME OBJECT *INTUITIONS*..."

"...AND IT IS *YOUR* JOB TO GATHER INTUITIONS OF THE *AUDITORY* SENSE, MR. BELL."

THE COURT HAS *ALREADY* HEARD TESTIMONY FROM YOUR COLLEAGUES AT *VISION STATION*... THE OL' *FACTORY*... *TASTETORIUM*... AND *TOUCH TERMINAL*...

...*NONE* OF THEM HAVE *EVER* RECEIVED INTUITIONS OF A *SUPREME BEING.*

HAVE *YOU?*

W-WELL... I...

NEED I REMIND YOU YOU ARE UNDER *OATH*, MR. BELL?

...NO, SIR.

THE HEARING PLANT HAS *NEVER* RECEIVED *ANY* SOUND INTUITIONS THAT THE DEFENDANT EXISTS IN TIME *OR* SPACE!

GASP!
MURMUR
WHISPER
MURMUR

38

THAT'S ENOUGH! *ORDER* IN THE COURT!

YOUR WITNESS, MR. KANT.

THE DEFENSE HAS *NO QUESTIONS* FOR THIS WITNESS, YOUR HONOR.

VERY WELL. MR. BELL, YOU ARE EXCUSED.

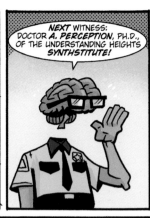

NEXT WITNESS: DOCTOR *A. PERCEPTION*, PH.D., OF THE UNDERSTANDING HEIGHTS *SYNTHSTITUTE!*

TELL THE JURY A LITTLE BIT ABOUT WHAT YOU *DO*, DOCTOR.

WELL... WE AT THE *SYNTHSTITUTE* LIKE TO SAY WE'RE IN THE *TRUTH* BUSINESS...

...WHICH IS THE "ACCORDANCE OF A *COGNITION* WITH ITS *OBJECT*."

"WHEN WE RECEIVE *INTUITIONS* FROM SENSUOUS FLATS, WE MATCH THEM WITH THE PROPER *CONCEPTION*."

HEARING PLANT

TICK-TOCK TICK-TOCK

ZZZz

"IN ORDER TO GET *KNOWLEDGE*, YOU CAN'T HAVE *ONE* WITHOUT THE *OTHER*!"

"IN A *SYNTHETICAL* COGNITION, YOU *AUGMENT* AN INTUITION WITH A CONCEPTION."

ZZZZ

meow.

TICK-TOCK TICK-TOCK

"OR, IN THE CASE OF AN *ANALYTICAL* COGNITION, THE CONCEPTION IS CONTAINED *WITHIN* THE INTUITION ITSELF..."

❶ ❷

❸

"...LIKE, YOU KNOW, A *TRIANGLE* IS BY *DEFINITION* A THREE-SIDED OBJECT."

JUST SO WE'RE *CLEAR*, DOCTOR: IS IT *NECESSARY* FOR THERE TO BE INCOMING *SENSE DATA* TO FORM *COGNITIONS*?

OHHH *NO*, NOT AT ALL!

"IN OUR *IMAGINATION* DEPARTMENT, WE CAN REPRESENT AN OBJECT EVEN *WITHOUT* ITS PRESENCE IN THE SENSES."

"AND, JUST AS WE RENDER SENSATIONS *INTELLIGIBLE*, WE ALSO RENDER ABSTRACT CONCEPTIONS *SENSUOUS* -- SUCH AS A *'LINE'*, WHICH DOES NOT EXIST IN *REALITY* UNTIL WE *MAKE* IT SO."

SINCE I LOST MY !@#$! *RULER* IT'S BEEN GETTIN' IN THE WAY OF MY *REALITY!!*

"*AND* OBJECTS CAN ORIGINATE FROM *INSIDE* THE MIND-- THESE ARE *'IDEAS'*, WHICH ARE NOT SENSE OBJECTS, BUT *NECESSARY* CONCEPTIONS OF *REASON*."

INTUITIONS

IDEAS

EGO

AND DO YOU SEE ANY SUCH *TRANSCENDENTAL OBJECTS* HERE IN THE COURTROOM TODAY?

YES, I DO...

...THE DEFENDANT!

LIES! ALL LIES!

I'VE *NEVER SEEN* THIS FACULTY OF COGNITION BEFORE IN MY LIFE!!

ORDER! ORDER!

BAILIFFS, RESTRAIN THE DEFENDANT!

NOW THAT I MAY PROCEED --AHEM!-- UNINTERRUPTED...

...I'D LIKE TO DRAW YOUR ATTENTION TO THE *COSMOLOGICAL* PROOF OF THE DEFENDANT'S EXISTENCE, DOCTOR.

"IN *THIS* TIDY BIT OF *SOPHISTRY*, IT IS ASSERTED THAT BECAUSE THE BIG I EXISTS, GOD *MUST* EXIST BY THE LAW OF *CAUSE-AND-EFFECT*...

THAT WITHOUT A *NECESSARY BEING* TO SET EXISTENCE IN MOTION IN THE *FIRST* PLACE, *NOTHING* WOULD EXIST AT ALL!"

"HOW WOULD *YOU* RESPOND?"

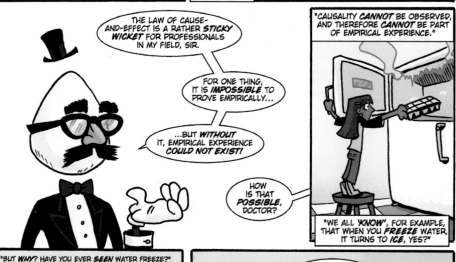

THE LAW OF CAUSE-AND-EFFECT IS A RATHER *STICKY WICKET* FOR PROFESSIONALS IN MY FIELD, SIR.

FOR ONE THING, IT IS *IMPOSSIBLE* TO PROVE EMPIRICALLY...

...BUT *WITHOUT* IT, EMPIRICAL EXPERIENCE *COULD NOT EXIST!*

HOW IS THAT *POSSIBLE*, DOCTOR?

"CAUSALITY *CANNOT* BE OBSERVED, AND THEREFORE *CANNOT* BE PART OF EMPIRICAL EXPERIENCE."

"WE ALL *KNOW*", FOR EXAMPLE, THAT WHEN YOU *FREEZE* WATER, IT TURNS TO *ICE*, YES?"

"BUT *WHY*? HAVE YOU EVER *SEEN* WATER FREEZE?"

GEEZ... THIS IS *BORING*... --YAWN!--

"OF *COURSE* NOT...YOU JUST GO AWAY, AND WHEN YOU COME BACK, IT'S ICE! THAT ESTABLISHES NO DEFINITIVE *CAUSAL* RELATIONSHIP--"

--NOR *CAN* YOU ESTABLISH ONE THROUGH THE *SENSES* ALONE!

MAY IT PLEASE THE COURT... PEOPLE'S EXHIBIT "A"!

A TABLE OF THE *A PRIORI CONCEPTIONS* OF THE UNDERSTANDING... THE *CATEGORIES!*

Of QUANTITY
Unity
Plurality
Totality
Of QUALITY
Reality
Negation
Limitation
"ALL A POSTERIORI INTUITIONS ARE MERGED WITH ONE OR MORE OF THESE A PRIORI CONCEPTIONS TO FORM UNDERSTANDING!"
Of RELATION
Inherence & Subsistence
Causality & Dependence
Community
Of MODALITY
Possibility
Existence
Necessity
Impossibility
Non-existence
Contingence
"ALL THE CATEGORIES RELATE TO SPACE AND/OR TIME."
"IN THE CASE OF FREEZING, TWO OBSERVATIONS LINKED IN THE SAME SPACE (FOR WATER AND ICE HAVE THE SAME SUBSTANCE) ACROSS SUCCESSIVE TIMES UNDER THE CONDITION OF COLD FALL INTO THE CAUSALITY & DEPENDENCE CATEGORY."
BUT, AS I SAID BEFORE, YOU CAN'T HAVE KNOWLEDGE WITHOUT BOTH AN INTUITION AND A CONCEPTION--
--YOU CANNOT APPLY A CATEGORY LIKE CAUSALITY TO A PURELY INTELLECTUAL CONCEPTION!
SUCH AS THE DEFENDANT-- WHOM WE HAVE ALREADY ESTABLISHED HAS NO SENSE DATA ASSOCIATED WITH HIM?
YES, PRECISELY!
MR. KANT?
MR. KANT!
HMH?
YOUR WITNESS, MR. KANT!
OH-- NO QUESTIONS, YOUR HONOR!
MMMMMFFF!!

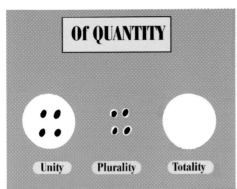

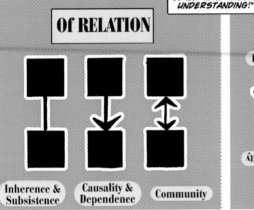

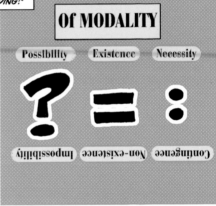

dum-DUM!

SUPREME COURT
PART 2,541
SUNDAY, JULY 31

THE *PHYSICO-THEOLOGICAL PROOF* IS ALSO KNOWN AS THE *"TELEOLOGICAL"* ONE.

THAT IS, SINCE THE SO-CALLED "NATURAL" WORLD MANIFESTS SIGNS OF PURPOSE OR *DESIGN*, IT MUST BE *DIRECTED* BY AN *INTELLIGENT, OMNIPOTENT BEING* LIKE THE DEFENDANT!

HOW WOULD YOU *RESPOND* TO THAT?

WELL GEE WHIZ, I THINK IT'S A THEORY THE BIG I REALLY SHOULD *CONSIDER*--

OF COURSE *YOU'D* THINK THAT. BECAUSE YOU'RE AN *IDIOT*.

AH-- PLEASE, YOU ARE *ONE* WITNESS, SO I NEED *ONE* ANSWER--

"*SHUCKS*, THAT'S NOT EASY FOR US TO *DO*, SIR! IN REASON TOWERS WE'RE AN *ANTIMONY*..."

GOSH, DON'T YOU THINK THE UNIVERSE HAS A BEGINNING IN *TIME* ... AND TOO, IS LIMITED IN *SPACE*?

ANY HALFWIT COULD SEE THAT THE UNIVERSE IS *ETERNAL* IN TIME AND *INFINITE* IN SPACE, YOU *NO-WIT*!

"--A *CONTRADICTORY*, BUT MUTUALLY *PROVABLE* PAIR OF CLAIMS THAT REASON IS *COMPELLED* TOWARD!"

YOU CAN RESOLVE AN ANTIMONY LIKE US ONLY BY UNDERSTANDING HOW THE BIG I'S REASON *ITSELF* ENHANCES...

...AND SOMETIMES *ALTERS* OUR EXPERIENCE OF OBJECTS!

"EVER NOTICE HOW WHEN A REALLY *TRAUMATIC* EVENT HAPPENS, PEOPLE SEE IT AS CONFIRMING WHAT THEY *ALREADY* BELIEVED TO BE TRUE IN THE *FIRST PLACE*?"

YOUR LIMP-WRISTED *ANTI-TERRORISM POLICY* GOT US *INTO* THIS MESS!

THESE ARE THE CHICKENS OF *YOUR* EXPLOITATIVE *FOREIGN POLICY* COMING HOME TO *ROOST*, MAN!

43

THAT'S BECAUSE, UNLESS WE'RE VIGILANT TO STOP IT, OUR REASON CAN IMPOSE *ARTIFICIAL PATTERNS* ON INCOMING DATA IN A MISGUIDED ATTEMPT TO RENDER THE *EXTERNAL* WORLD AS ORDERLY AS OUR *INTERNAL* ONE!

TAKE *CONSPIRACY THEORY*, FOR INSTANCE. THE POPULAR ON-LINE DOCUMENTARY *LOOSE CHANGE* (LOOSECHANGE911.COM) CONTENDS THAT THESE *SINISTER-SEEMING* FACTS FORM A *DAMNING PATTERN*:

IN SEPTEMBER 2000, CONSERVATIVE THINK TANK *PROJECT FOR A NEW AMERICAN CENTURY* (WHOSE MEMBERS INCLUDE *DICK CHENEY, DONALD RUMSFELD, JEB BUSH,* AND OTHER *BUSHIES*) WRITE THAT *"ANOTHER PEARL HARBOR"* IS NECESSARY TO REBUILD AMERICA'S DEFENSES.

THAT *OCTOBER,* THE PENTAGON SIMULATES A BOEING 757 SMASHING INTO A *BUILDING.*

AND LESS THAN FOUR MONTHS PRIOR TO 9/11, THE OWNER OF THE TWIN TOWERS TOOK OUT A $3.5 BILLION TERRORISM *INSURANCE POLICY* ON THE W.T.C.!

BUT NEW AMERICAN CENTURY NEVER SAID AMERICA NEEDED TO *ENGINEER* SUCH AN ATTACK IN ORDER TO REJIGGER THE MILITARY!

UM...HEY...DOESN'T THE MILITARY HAVE, LIKE, *MISSILES* AND *BOMBS* AND STUFF TO KNOCK DOWN BUILDINGS? WOULDN'T THEY SIMULATE A CRASH JUST TO TRAIN *RESPONSES* TO IT?

SINCE TERRORISTS HAD ALREADY *TRIED* TO BLOW UP THE W.T.C. IN *1993,* DON'T YOU THINK GETTING INSURANCE OUT AGAINST IT HAPPENING *AGAIN* IS A PRETTY GOOD IDEA?

SO... IT IS *YOUR* CONTENTION THAT *"INTELLIGENT DESIGN"* IS CUT FROM THE SAME CLOTH AS *CONSPIRACY THEORY:* ANOTHER EXAMPLE OF REASON'S TENDENCY TO *OVERREACH*--TO MAKE *CONNECTIONS* WHERE THERE *ARE NONE?*

THAT'S SOMETHING WE *BOTH* CAN AGREE ON!

WAIT, NO, LET ME *GUESS*-- YOU HAVE *NO QUESTIONS* FOR THIS WITNESS!

HEY, YOU REALLY *ARE* OMNISCIENT!

SEEING AS HOW THE DEFENSE HAS NOT SEEN FIT TO CROSS-EXAMINE *ANY* OF MY WITNESSES...

...THE PROSECUTION *RESTS*!

THE FLOOR IS *YOURS*, MR. KANT. AND I MUST SAY YOUR *INACTIVITY* UP UNTIL THIS POINT HAS GIVEN YOUR CLIENT *EXCELLENT* GROUNDS FOR APPEAL DUE TO *INCOMPETENT COUNSEL*--

MY *WITNESS LIST*, YOUR HONOR!

BUT... THERE'S ONLY *ONE NAME* HERE!

THAT'S BECAUSE THE ONLY ENTITY I NEED TO CALL...

...IS PURE SPECULATIVE REASONING *ITSELF*!

GASP!

SO IT IS YOUR ASSERTION THAT EMPIRICAL KNOWLEDGE IS A *COMPOUND* OF THAT WHICH WE RECEIVE THROUGH *IMPRESSIONS*, AND THAT WHICH THE FACULTY OF COGNITION SUPPLIES FROM *ITSELF*?

SO GLAD YOU'VE BEEN PAYING *ATTENTION*!

IS THAT A *YES* OR A *NO*?

YES, OF COURSE YES!

BUT *WHAT*, I ASK YOU, IS THE NATURE OF OBJECTS CONSIDERED AS THINGS *IN THEMSELVES*, *WITHOUT* REFERENCE TO THE RECEPTIVITY OF OUR SENSIBILITY?

WELL, I, ER--

YOU DON'T *KNOW*, DO YOU?!

JUST GIVE ME A SECOND TO THIN--

ANSWER THE QUESTION!!

45

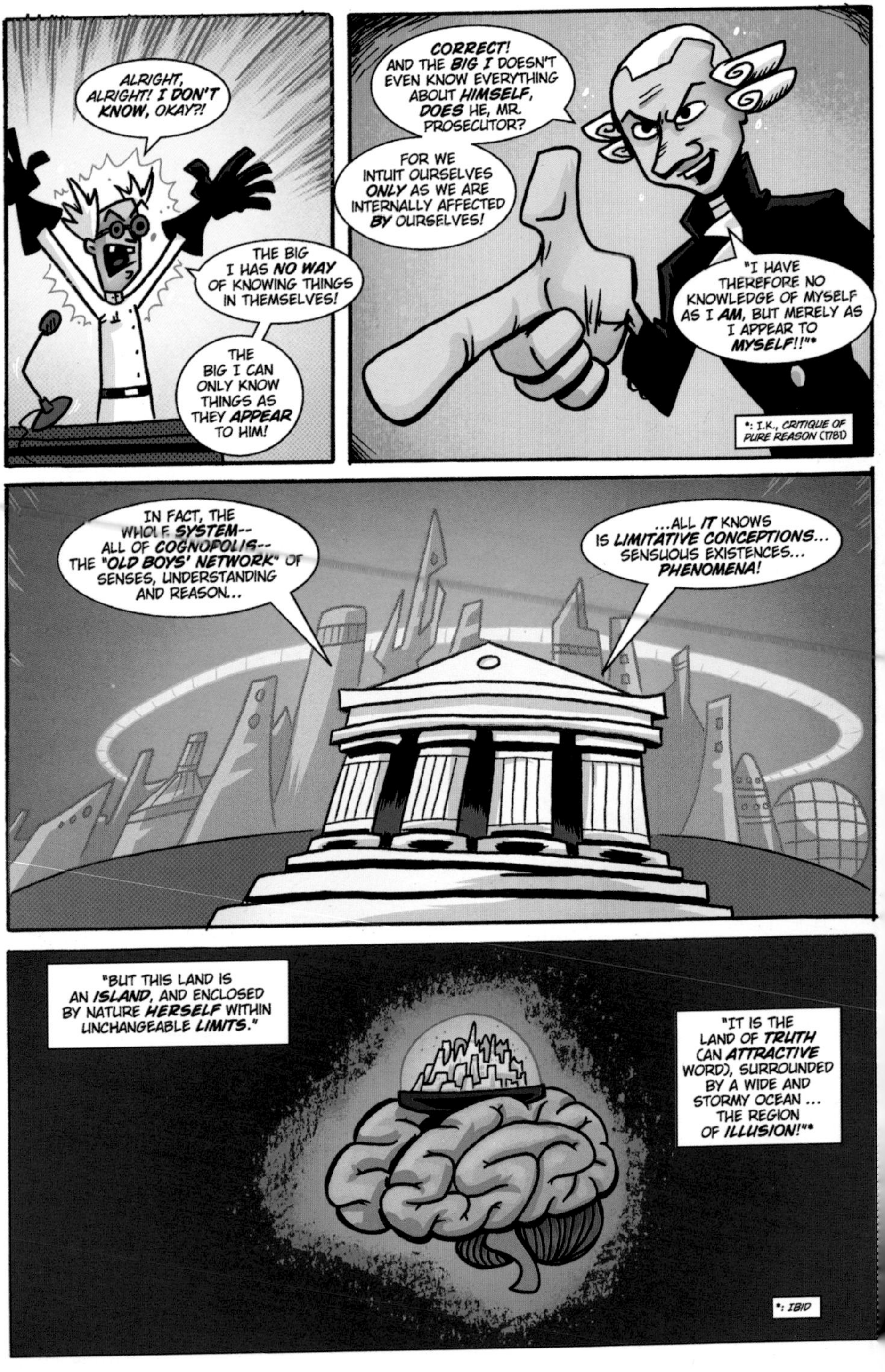

ALRIGHT, ALRIGHT! I DON'T KNOW, OKAY?!
THE BIG I HAS NO WAY OF KNOWING THINGS IN THEMSELVES!
THE BIG I CAN ONLY KNOW THINGS AS THEY APPEAR TO HIM!
CORRECT! AND THE BIG I DOESN'T EVEN KNOW EVERYTHING ABOUT HIMSELF, DOES HE, MR. PROSECUTOR?
FOR WE INTUIT OURSELVES ONLY AS WE ARE INTERNALLY AFFECTED BY OURSELVES!
"I HAVE THEREFORE NO KNOWLEDGE OF MYSELF AS I AM, BUT MERELY AS I APPEAR TO MYSELF!!"*
*: I.K., CRITIQUE OF PURE REASON (1781)
IN FACT, THE WHOLE SYSTEM-- ALL OF COGNOPOLIS-- THE "OLD BOYS' NETWORK" OF SENSES, UNDERSTANDING AND REASON...
...ALL IT KNOWS IS LIMITATIVE CONCEPTIONS... SENSUOUS EXISTENCES... PHENOMENA!
"BUT THIS LAND IS AN ISLAND, AND ENCLOSED BY NATURE HERSELF WITHIN UNCHANGEABLE LIMITS."
"IT IS THE LAND OF TRUTH (AN ATTRACTIVE WORD), SURROUNDED BY A WIDE AND STORMY OCEAN ... THE REGION OF ILLUSION!"*
*: IBID

"*NOUMENAL* REALITY -- *NON-SENSUAL* REALITY -- WILL ALWAYS BE LITTLE MORE THAN A SOURCE OF CONJECTURE AND *SPECULATION* TO THE BIG I."

NOW SHOWING

IT CAME FROM NOUMENA!

ISN'T IT *TRUE*, MR. PROSECUTOR, THAT *ALL* SPECULATIVE REASON CAN PROVE IS THAT A SUPREME AND ALL-SUFFICIENT BEING LIKE MY CLIENT, *IF* HE EXISTS, IS *NOUMENAL* -- *BEYOND* THE REALM OF SENSUOUS EXPERIENCE...

...WHICH IS *EXACTLY* WHAT *HE* HAS MAINTAINED ALL *ALONG?*

IN OTHER WORDS...WHILE THE BIG I CANNOT PROVE THAT MY CLIENT *EXISTS...*

...HE CANNOT PROVE HE DOES *NOT* EXIST, EITHER!

IS THAT NOT *RIGHT*, SIR?

YES.

THE DEFENSE *RESTS!*

dum-DUM!

CLOSING STATEMENTS
MONDAY, MARCH 4

LADIES AND GENTLEMEN OF THE *JURY*...

THE PROSECUTOR IS *RIGHT* WHEN HE SAYS THAT, AS A MATTER OF *PURE REASON*, WE DO NOT HAVE THE *SLIGHTEST GROUND* TO ASSUME IN AN *ABSOLUTE MANNER* THAT THE *OBJECT* OF THE IDEA OF A SUPREME BEING IS MY *CLIENT*.

"BUT REASON IS *NOT* THE END-ALL AND BE-ALL OF LIFE! WE CANNOT ALLOW IT AND ITS OFFSPRING, *SCIENCE*, CREATE A *CLOCKWORK WORLD* WHERE HUMAN FREEDOM HAS NO *PLACE*."

"*WHERE* IN MR. PROSECUTOR'S WORLD IS THERE ROOM FOR SUCH A THING AS *HAPPINESS*--THE CONDITION OF A RATIONAL BEING *IN* THE WORLD, IN WHOSE WHOLE *EXISTENCE* EVERYTHING GOES ACCORDING TO *WISH* AND *WILL*?"

GOIN' *CHOPPY-CHOP* MAKES *ME* HAPPY!

NOT SO *FAST*, MY HOMICIDAL FRIEND!

I, GOD, AM THE IDEAL OF THE *HIGHEST GOOD* (*SUMMUM BONUM*) AGAINST WHICH ALL *LEGITIMATE HAPPINESS* MUST BE *MEASURED*!

AND *I* SAY AXE MURDERS *AIN'T* GOOD!

THE *HIGHEST* GOOD IS POSSIBLE IN THE WORLD *ONLY* ON THE SUPPOSITION OF A *SUPREME CAUSE OF NATURE* WHICH HAS A CAUSALITY CORRESPONDING TO THE *MORAL* DISPOSITION.

tik tik

"THEREFORE, IT IS *MORALLY NECESSARY* TO ASSUME THE EXISTENCE OF *MY CLIENT*!"*

*: I.K., *CRITIQUE OF PRACTICAL REASON* (1788)

48

HAS THE JURY REACHED A **VERDICT**?

WE **HAVE**, YOUR HONOR.

WE THE JURY, ON THE **SOLE** COUNT OF THE INDICTMENT, FIND THE DEFENDANT...

...THE CREATOR AND ARCHITECT OF THE **UNIVERSE**, THE SUPREME, ALL-SUFFICIENT AND **NECESSARY** BEING...

...**NOT GUILTY** BEYOND A REASONABLE DOUBT OF **NOT EXISTING**!

YES!

THANK YOU, MR. KANT! I COULDN'T HAVE DONE IT **WITHOUT** YOU.

MY PLEASURE, SIR. ANY TIME.

AND HERE'S MY **BILL**!

WHA--

AAAGGHH!!

GOD IS **DEAD**!

BA-DUMP-BUMP!

Once upon a time...
(the 1820s)

...in a school far, far away...

(the University of Berlin)

There lived two professors...

GEORG W. F. HEGEL
(Action Philosopher #24)

ARTHUR SCHOPENHAUER
(Action Philosopher #25)

KANT

...and they BOTH thought

IMMANUEL KANT

was the greatest philosopher EVER!

SYNTHESIS (COMIC) = **THESIS** (FRED VAN LENTE) + **ANTITHESIS** (RYAN DUNLAVEY)	**OR**	WORLD (COMIC) = **IDEA** (FRED VAN LENTE) + **REPRESENTATION** (RYAN DUNLAVEY)

Nevertheless, they BOTH disagreed with Kant's assertion that Things-in-THEMSELVES were fundamentally UNKNOWABLE.

From there, however...

Their paths RADICALLY DIVERGED...

GEORG SAID...

EVERYTHING THAT *IS*, IS *KNOWABLE!*

FOR KNOWING AND BEING ARE JUST *TWO SIDES* OF THE *SAME COIN!*

IN FACT, FOR HEGEL, EVERY THING (*THESIS*) ALSO CONTAINS ITS OPPOSITE (*ANTITHESIS*)!

TAKE THE CONCEPT OF *"BEING"*: WITHOUT THE CONCEPT OF *"NOTHING"*, "BEING" MAKES NO *SENSE*, FOR WHAT IS A SOMETHING EXCEPT A *NOT-NOTHING?*

BEE-ING

NOT BEE-ING

AND WHAT IS *NOTHING* EXCEPT NOT-*SOMETHING?*

BY THINKING ABOUT *BEING*, YOU *ALSO* HAVE TO THINK ABOUT *NON-BEING* -- AND *VICE-VERSA* -- BECAUSE YOU CAN'T DEFINE THE *ONE* WITHOUT *INVOKING* THE *OTHER*.

DUUUDE!! I CAN *FLIP IT* WITH MY *MIND!*

THIS PERPETUAL LOOP OF *COGNITIVE MOTION* PRODUCES A *THIRD* CATEGORY, A *SYNTHESIS* OF THE TWO THAT GEORG CALLED...

... *"BECOMING!"*

WHICH IS NOT QUITE *NOTHING*, BUT NOT QUITE SOMETHING, EITHER -- IT'S *IN-BETWEEN!*

BECAUSE *ALL* OF REALITY IS IN A PROCESS OF *BECOMING*...

OBJECTS-IN-THEMSELVES ARE NOTHING LESS THAN THE SUM OF THE *THOUGHTS* WE HAVE ABOUT THEM!

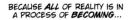

wood

Shaker

brown

3.5 ft. high

made in Wisconsin

37 years old

from Sears

for sitting

four-legged

used to be in Mom's house

NOT ONLY IS APPEARANCE ALSO *REALITY*...

...BUT REALITY IS *RATIONAL*, FOLLOWING THE LOGIC OF MY *TRIADIC DIALECTIC!*

"WHAT IS RATIONAL IS REAL, WHAT IS REAL, IS RATIONAL!"

SUGAR

KANT TOUCH THIS

1 2 3
1 2 3

GEORG REACHED *HIS* CONCLUSIONS BY BEGINNING WITH THE *LOWEST* LEVEL OF KNOWLEDGE-- *SENSE PERCEPTIONS, ETC.*--

--POSING A *THESIS,* DEDUCING ITS *ANTITHESIS,* THEN FINDING *THEIR* UNITY IN A HIGHER *SYNTHESIS!*

FOR *SINGLE* FACTS ARE *"IRRATIONAL"* BY THEMSELVES; THEY MUST BE CONSIDERED WITHIN *CONTEXT* OF THE *WHOLE!*

THIS IS A *TREE!*

THIS IS A *SNAKE!*

THIS IS *HARASSMENT!*

AT THE *END* OF THIS CHAIN OF CONCLUSIONS ONE FINDS THE *IDEA*--

--WHICH IS THE SYNTHESIS OF *SUBJECTIVITY* (THESIS) AND *OBJECTIVITY* (ANTITHESIS)!

"KANT WAS *WRONG* TO THINK HIS *CATEGORIES* WERE MERE *FIGMENTS* OF *REASON!* NO, THEY ARE MODES OF *BEING* THAT EXIST *IN* THE WORLD!"

AND THE SYNTHESIS OF *BEING* (THESIS) AND *COGNITION* (ANTITHESIS) IS THE *ABSOLUTE IDEA,* WHICH ALL OTHER IDEAS MOVE *TOWARD...*

...IN A PROCESS OF *PERFECTION* BY WHICH THE *ABSOLUTE* FULLY *KNOWS* ITSELF *IN* OBJECTS!

ARTHUR SAID...

...WHILE KANT IS **ESSENTIALLY** RIGHT ABOUT THE UNKNOWABILITY OF THINGS-IN-THEMSELVES, WE DO HAVE **ONE** NARROW DOOR INTO THEIR NATURE...

...BECAUSE THAT DOOR IS **WITHIN** EACH AND EVERY **ONE** OF US!

THAT "DOOR" IS OUR **BODILY ACTIONS**, WHICH WE USUALLY ASSUME TO BE MERELY **INSTIGATED** BY OUR **DESIRES** -- OUR **WILL**!

I WANT IT I WANT IT I **WANT** IT!!

USED

NO-FRIENDO SEX-BOX 720™

NEW!

BUT ARTHUR POINTS OUT THAT IT IS ONLY UPON **REFLECTION** THAT THERE IS A **CAUSAL** RELATIONSHIP BETWEEN WILL AND ACTION.

No-FRIEND SEX-BOX 720

RATHER, HE WRITES, "THE ACTION OF THE BODY IS NOTHING BUT THE ACT OF THE WILL **OBJECTIFIED!**"

=

"THE ACT OF WILL IS...THE CLOSEST AND MOST DISTINCT **MANIFESTATION** OF THE THING-IN-ITSELF! WE OURSELVES **ARE** THE THING-IN-ITSELF!"

THINGS-IN-THEMSELVES **ARE** WILL...

...OR, MORE **PRECISELY**, THERE IS ONLY **ONE** WILL, AND THINGS-IN-THE-WORLD ARE INDIVIDUAL MANIFESTATIONS OF THAT WILL!

ARTHUR REACHED *HIS* CONCLUSIONS...

...BECAUSE THE *PRINCIPLE OF SUFFICIENT REASON* SHOWS US THAT EVERYWHERE IS PRESENT *NECESSITY!*

TO HAVE PHYSICAL OBJECTS, A/K/A *PHENOMENA*, YOU NEED *CAUSE-AND-EFFECT!*

ABSTRACT CONCEPTS DEMAND INFERENCE OR *IMPLICATION!*

MATH REQUIRES *TIME* (WITHOUT *SEQUENCE* YOU CAN'T *COUNT*)...

FREEDOM

...AND *SPACE* (FOR *GEOMETRY*)!

"AND FOR THERE TO BE A *SELF*, THERE NEEDS TO BE AN ASPECT OF YOU THAT *YOU* OBSERVE ... AN *OBJECT*-YOU TO GO WITH THE *SUBJECT*-YOU!"

WILLING *Subject*

NO-FRIENDO SEX-BOX **720**

KNOWING *Subject*

"THE SELF IS THE SUBJECT THAT *WILLS* AND THE *WILLING SUBJECT* IS THE OBJECT FOR THAT *KNOWING* SUBJECT!"

EVERYTHING IN THE WORLD (INCLUDING *YOU*) IS PRESENTED TO YOUR MIND AS AN *OBJECT* TO A *SUBJECT*.

ARTHUR CONCLUDES, "THE WHOLE WORLD OF OBJECTS IS AND REMAINS *REPRESENTATION*, AND THEREFORE FOREVER DETERMINED BY THE *SUBJECT*."

HENCE THE TITLE OF ARTHUR'S MOST FAMOUS WORK:

NO-FRIENDO SEX-BOX

*THE WORLD AS WILL AND REPRESENTATION.**

*: *"VORSTELLUNG"* IN GERMAN, WHICH IN ENGLISH IS FREQUENTLY (MIS-) TRANSLATED MORE SIMPLISTICALLY AS *"IDEA"*.

GEORG SAID...

...THE WORLD-- *NATURE*--IS THE EXTERNAL/ *CORPOREAL* FORM (ANTITHESIS) OF THE *IDEA* (SYNTHESIS)!

THE SYNTHESIS OF *IDEA* AND *NATURE* IS *GEIST* ("SPIRIT" OR "*MIND*"), A RATHER *SLIPPERY* CONCEPT THAT APPEARS TO BE TO HUMAN *BEHAVIOR* WHAT "*BEING*" IS TO GEORG'S *METAPHYSICS*:

A STATE OF HIGHEST *ABSTRACTION* IN "THE REALM OF *FREEDOM*."

JUST AS INDIVIDUAL *THINGS* EMANATE FROM FORMLESS *BEING*, SO INDIVIDUAL MOMENTS IN *HISTORY* EMANATE FROM *SPIRIT*.

AND JUST AS THE ABSOLUTE IDEA IS IN A NEVER-ENDING PROCESS OF *ACTUALIZATION*, HISTORY ITSELF IS IN A NEVER-ENDING FORWARD *ADVANCEMENT* TOWARD PERFECT EXPRESSION IN *ABSOLUTE SPIRIT*!

IN *RELIGION*, FOR EXAMPLE, WE BEGAN WITH AMORPHOUS *ANIMISM* (THESIS), WHICH MOVED TO PAGAN *ANTHROPOMORPHISM* (ANTITHESIS) -- IN WHICH *SPECIFIC* DEITIES EMBODY *SPECIFIC* ASPECTS OF CREATION -- CULMINATING IN *CHRISTIANITY* (SYNTHESIS), IN WHICH *ALL* OF CREATION IS EMBODIED IN ONE, *INDIVIDUAL* DEITY!

LIKEWISE, THE *STATE*, IN GEORG'S VIEW, IS *NOT* CREATED BY MAN, BUT EMANATES FROM DIALECTIC MOVEMENTS OF *HISTORY*!

"THE STATE IS THE *ACTUALITY* OF THE *ETHICAL IDEA*," HE WROTE, AN *ORGANISM* STRIVING TOWARD *MAXIMUM FREEDOM*.

AND SO IT MOVED FROM *TYRANNY* (THESIS) TO *DEMOCRACY* (ANTITHESIS) TO EUROPEAN-STYLE *MONARCHY* (SYNTHESIS)!

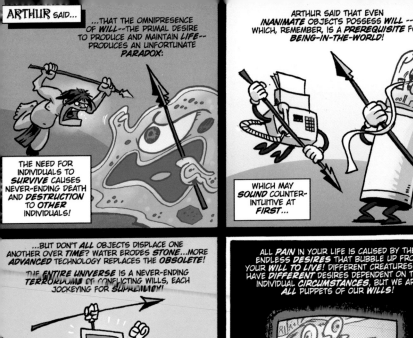

ARTHUR said...

...THAT THE OMNIPRESENCE OF **WILL**--THE PRIMAL DESIRE TO PRODUCE AND MAINTAIN **LIFE**--PRODUCES AN UNFORTUNATE **PARADOX:**

THE NEED FOR INDIVIDUALS TO **SURVIVE** CAUSES NEVER-ENDING DEATH AND **DESTRUCTION** TO **OTHER** INDIVIDUALS!

ARTHUR SAID THAT EVEN **INANIMATE** OBJECTS POSSESS **WILL** -- WHICH, REMEMBER, IS A **PREREQUISITE** FOR **BEING-IN-THE-WORLD!**

WHICH MAY **SOUND** COUNTER-INTUITIVE AT **FIRST...**

...BUT DON'T **ALL** OBJECTS DISPLACE ONE ANOTHER OVER **TIME?** WATER ERODES **STONE**...MORE **ADVANCED** TECHNOLOGY REPLACES THE **OBSOLETE!**

THE **ENTIRE UNIVERSE** IS A NEVER-ENDING **TERRORDOME** OF CONFLICTING WILLS, EACH JOCKEYING FOR **SUPREMACY!**

ALL **PAIN** IN YOUR LIFE IS CAUSED BY THE ENDLESS **DESIRES** THAT BUBBLE UP FROM YOUR **WILL TO LIVE!** DIFFERENT CREATURES MAY HAVE **DIFFERENT** DESIRES DEPENDENT ON THEIR INDIVIDUAL **CIRCUMSTANCES,** BUT WE ARE **ALL** PUPPETS OF OUR **WILLS!**

DON'T CARE | MILD INTEREST | WANT CONSOLE! | ROB STORE

OH MY **GAWD!** YOU'RE SO, LIKE, **PESSIMISTIC!**

BAH! WHAT **YOU** CALL PESSIMISM IS "AN OBJECTIVE **RECOGNITION** OF FOLLY AND **MALEVOLENCE!"***

*: ACTUAL QUOTE!

ARTHUR WAS **UNIQUE** AMONG PHILOSOPHERS IN BELIEVING THAT HUMANITY'S **INTELLECT** WAS NO BETTER -- OR **DIFFERENT** -- THAN THE INSTINCTS OF **ANIMALS.**

"RATIONALITY" IS SUSTAINED ONLY FOR **BRIEF** PERIODS OF TIME -- WHILE THE WILL **PERPETUALLY** DRIVES US!

"ALBERT" HOMO SAPIENS

(YOU MIGHT NOT BE **SHOCKED** TO HEAR THAT ARTHUR WAS A **VEGETARIAN.**)

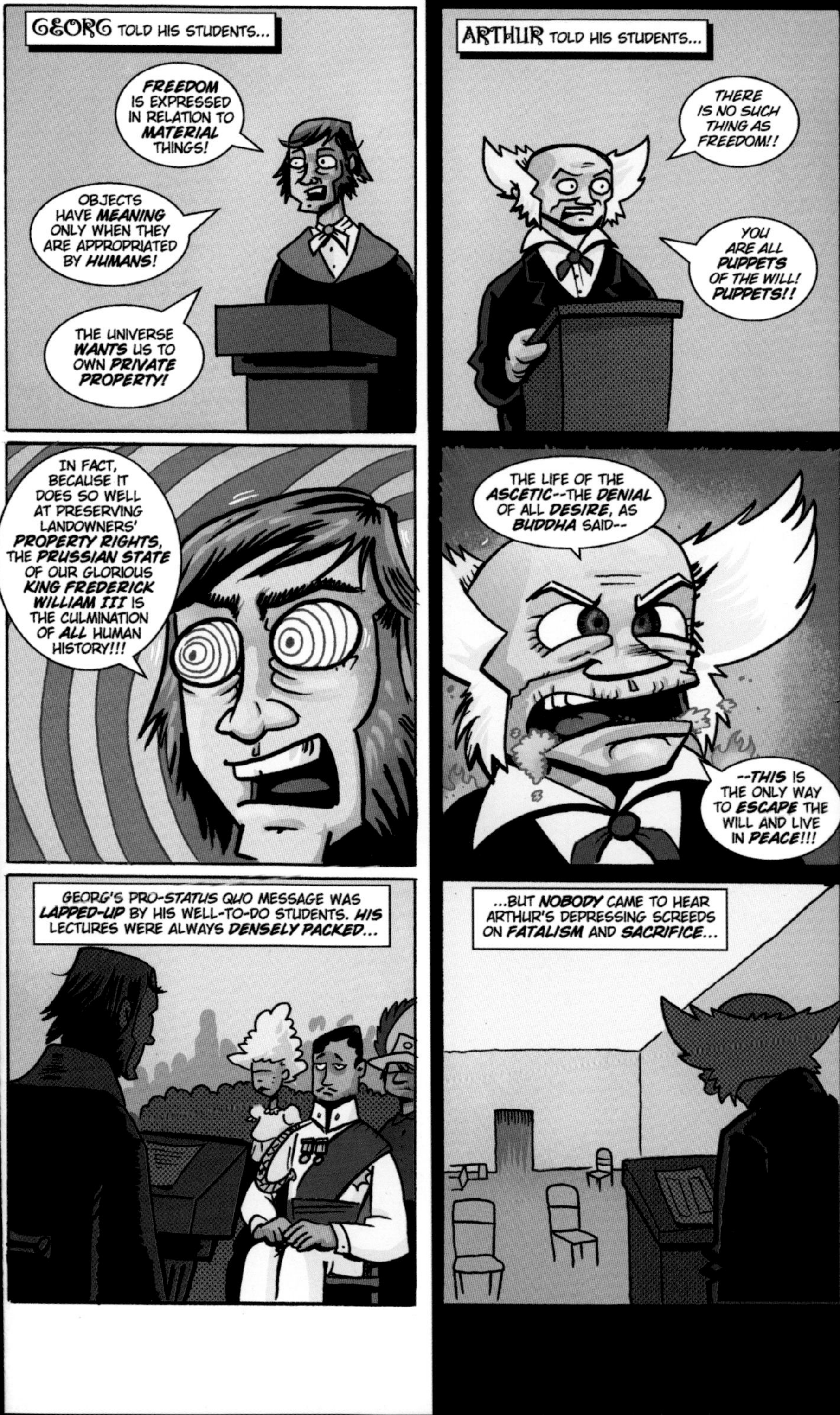
GEORG TOLD HIS STUDENTS...
FREEDOM IS EXPRESSED IN RELATION TO MATERIAL THINGS!
OBJECTS HAVE MEANING ONLY WHEN THEY ARE APPROPRIATED BY HUMANS!
THE UNIVERSE WANTS US TO OWN PRIVATE PROPERTY!
ARTHUR TOLD HIS STUDENTS...
THERE IS NO SUCH THING AS FREEDOM!!
YOU ARE ALL PUPPETS OF THE WILL! PUPPETS!!
IN FACT, BECAUSE IT DOES SO WELL AT PRESERVING LANDOWNERS' PROPERTY RIGHTS, THE PRUSSIAN STATE OF OUR GLORIOUS KING FREDERICK WILLIAM III IS THE CULMINATION OF ALL HUMAN HISTORY!!!
THE LIFE OF THE ASCETIC--THE DENIAL OF ALL DESIRE, AS BUDDHA SAID--
--THIS IS THE ONLY WAY TO ESCAPE THE WILL AND LIVE IN PEACE!!!
GEORG'S PRO-STATUS QUO MESSAGE WAS LAPPED-UP BY HIS WELL-TO-DO STUDENTS. HIS LECTURES WERE ALWAYS DENSELY PACKED...
...BUT NOBODY CAME TO HEAR ARTHUR'S DEPRESSING SCREEDS ON FATALISM AND SACRIFICE...

...IN *PART*, ONE MUST ASSUME, BECAUSE BERLIN U. SCHEDULED THEIR LECTURES FOR THE *EXACT SAME TIME!*

ARTHUR DIDN'T APPRECIATE THAT TOO MUCH:

"IF I WERE TO SAY THAT THE SO-CALLED *PHILOSOPHY* OF THIS FELLOW *HEGEL* IS A COLOSSAL PIECE OF *MYSTIFICATION*"...

"...WITH AN INEXHAUSTIBLE THEME FOR *LAUGHTER* AT OUR TIMES, THAT IT IS A *PSEUDO*-PHILOSOPHY *PARALYZING* ALL MENTAL POWERS, STIFLING ALL *REAL* THINKING..."

"...I SHOULD BE *QUITE RIGHT!*"*

THE HA-HA HOLE

"*FURTHER*, IF I WERE TO SAY THAT THIS *SUMMUS PHILOSOPHUS* SCRIBBLED *NONSENSE* QUITE UNLIKE *ANY MORTAL BEFORE HIM*..."

"SO THAT WHOEVER COULD READ HIM WITHOUT FEELING AS IF HE WERE IN A *MADHOUSE*, WOULD QUALIFY AS AN INMATE FOR *BEDLAM*, I SHOULD BE NO *LESS* RIGHT!"*

ASYLUM

"THE HEIGHT OF *AUDACITY* IN ... STRINGING TOGETHER SENSELESS AND EXTRAVAGANT *MAZES* OF WORDS...WAS FINALLY REACHED IN *HEGEL*...WITH A RESULT WHICH WILL APPEAR *FABULOUS* TO POSTERITY..."

"...AS A *MONUMENT* TO *GERMAN STUPIDITY!*"*

DUMMHEIT

"OUT OF EVERY *PAGE* OF *HUME'S* THERE IS MORE TO BE LEARNED THAN OUT OF *ALL* OF THE PHILOSOPHICAL WORKS OF *HEGEL!*"*

(*: ALL *ACTUAL* QUOTES, NATCH.)

HEGEL

AS FOR WHAT *GEORG* THOUGHT ABOUT *ARTHUR*...

UM...

ARTHUR *WHO?*

HE'S THE GUY WITH THE *FUNNY HAIR*, RIGHT...?

MUCH HAS BEEN MADE OF THE FACT THAT GEORG WAS ONE OF THE ONLY MAJOR PHILOSOPHERS SINCE ANCIENT TIMES TO ACTUALLY GET MARRIED.

THE STATE IS BUT THE SYNTHESIS OF THE FAMILY (THESIS) AND CIVIL SOCIETY (ANTITHESIS)!

ARTHUR SHUNNED HUMAN CONTACT AND SLEPT WITH A PISTOL.

HE WAS SO PARANOID HE DID ALL HIS OWN SHAVING BECAUSE "I WOULDN'T TRUST MY NECK TO ANOTHER MAN'S RAZOR."

GEORG WAS SO POPULAR, HIS FOLLOWERS SPLIT INTO CONSERVATIVE RIGHT HEGELIANS, WHO SUPPORTED THE PRUSSIAN MONARCHY...AND RADICAL LEFT HEGELIANS LIKE KARL MARX, WHO WANTED A REVOLUTIONARY SYNTHESIS OUT OF THE GOVERNMENTS OF THE PAST!

ARTHUR SAID THAT THE ONLY THREE CHARACTERS IN HISTORY WORTH KNOWING WERE BUDDHA, KANT, AND HIS PET POODLE.

"I FEEL MOST AT HOME AMONG DEMIGODS AND DOGS."

"THEY ALONE ARE FREE FROM THE FAILINGS OF MEN!"

WHEN A CHOLERA EPIDEMIC SWEPT THROUGH BERLIN IN 1831, GEORG SUCCUMBED TO THE PLAGUE. SUPPOSEDLY HIS LAST WORDS WERE:

"ONLY ONE MAN EVER UNDERSTOOD ME."

"AND HE DIDN'T UNDERSTAND ME." ~GAK!~

BUT ARTHUR, WHO WAS TERRIFIED OF DISEASE, FLED THE CITY AS SOON AS THE PANDEMIC STARTED AND LIVED FOR ANOTHER THREE DECADES!

MY ASS IS OBJECTIFYING MY WILL TO GET THE HELL OUTTA HERE!

BERLIN

WHO GOT THE BETTER OF THE OTHER? YOU DECIDE!

BY THE POWER INVESTED IN ME, *HIGH PRIEST OF SCIENCE* AND ACTION PHILOSOPHER #27:

AUGUSTE COMTE!

...I HEREBY "INITIATE" YOU INTO THE *RELIGION OF HUMANITY*!!

NU-UH! 'CAUSE WE'RE NOTHING LIKE *CATHOLICISM*!

NOT ONE BIT!

WHICH IS SO TOTALLY *NOT A* CONFIRMATION!

TODAY'S BENEDICTION WILL BE DELIVERED BY
FRED VAN LENTE
ARCHBISHOP OF VERBAL HUMOR
RYAN DUNLAVEY
PATRON SAINT OF AMUSING DRAWINGS

YOUNG COMTE SERVED AS SECRETARY FOR FAMED FRENCH UTOPIAN THINKER *COUNT DE SAINT-SIMON* FOR SEVEN YEARS UNTIL A *POINTED BREAK* IN 1824.

ONLY BY ERADICATING *GREED* THROUGH *EDUCATION* CAN WE FORM THE PERFECT SOCIETY!

I CAN'T STAND YOUR INTELLECTUAL *PIPEDREAMS* ANY LONGER!

SOCIETY IS IN *REAL* CRISIS-- AND NEEDS *REAL* SOLUTIONS!!

COMTE BELIEVED THAT THE WAVE OF INSTABILITY AND VIOLENCE SWEEPING THROUGH EUROPE IN THE EARLY 19TH CENTURY WAS A DIRECT RESULT OF RELIGION'S RECENT *ASS-WHOOPING* BY SCIENCE.

GIMME YOUR LUNCH MONEY! *HAW!*

SHOVE!

SPLAT!

NEVERTHELESS, COMTE SAW THIS AS A *NATURAL EVOLUTION* IN THOUGHT, GUIDED BY WHAT HE CALLED *"THE LAW OF THREE STAGES"*:

STAGE 1: THEOLOGICAL!
PHENOMENA ARE EXPLAINED THROUGH THE SUPERNATURAL!

I CREATED MAN FROM *DUST* AND WOMAN FROM *MAN!*

WHY DO YOU SMELL LIKE *RIBS?*

MONCH, GNOSH! NO REASON...

STAGE 2: METAPHYSICAL!
MUCH THE SAME AS STAGE ONE, BUT THE SUPERNATURAL IS REPRESENTED AS ABSTRACT OR IMPERSONAL "FORCES!"

"NATURE" HAS CREATED ALL MEN *EQUAL!*

AND *WOMEN* TOO!

WELL, YES, I SUPPOSE, BUT MORE STUDIES NEED TO BE DONE... ~COUGH!~

STAGE 3: POSITIVISTIC!
PHENOMENA ARE EXPLAINED BY FORMULATION OF *SCIENTIFIC LAWS* BASED ON OBSERVING RELATIONS BETWEEN THEM! ANY ATTEMPT TO DISCOVER THE "ESSENCE" OR "SECRET CAUSES" OF THINGS IS *ABANDONED!*

EXCEPT FOR THE OBVIOUS *BIOLOGICAL* DIFFERENCES, MEN AND WOMEN ARE BASICALLY THE *SAME!*

GLAD WE COULD CLEAR THAT UP... *GROAN!*

NEWTON AND *GALILEO* HAD ALREADY BROUGHT *PHYSICS* AND *ASTRONOMY* INTO THE POSITIVE STAGE, RESPECTIVELY.

COMTE PLANNED TO DO THE *SAME* FOR THE *OTHER* REALMS OF HUMAN THOUGHT!

COMTE CALLED HIS THEORY OF INTERHUMAN RELATIONSHIPS *"SOCIOLOGY,"* AND DEEMED IT "THE *QUEEN* OF THE SCIENCES" BECAUSE ALL OTHER SPHERES OF KNOWLEDGE FED *INTO* IT.

HE BELIEVED SOCIOLOGY WAS ALL THAT STOOD AGAINST A *DESPOT* SEIZING CONTROL OF CIVIL SOCIETY IN THE VACUUM LEFT BY RELIGION'S DEFEAT.

COMTE HAD NO INTEREST IN BRINGING THE OLD RELIGION *BACK*, THOUGH -- HE'S *GLAD* IT WAS DEFEATED! BUT HE FELT SOCIETY NEEDED THE STRUCTURE AND *COMFORT* RELIGION PROVIDES!

NO, NO-- TOO *COMPLICATED!*

IKEA RELIJON

UNLIKE MANY REFORMERS OF HIS DAY, COMTE BELIEVED A RADICAL RECONSTRUCTION OF SOCIAL INSTITUTIONS WAS *IMPRACTICAL* AND CREATED PROHIBITIVE *DISRUPTION.*

COMTE WOULD *GRAFT* HUMANISTIC IDEALS ONTO THE *PREEXISTING* RELIGIOUS STRUCTURE!

INSTEAD OF AN *IMAGINARY* GOD, WE WILL WORSHIP *HUMANITY* ITSELF...

...BUT BY "WORSHIP," I MEAN MIRROR *HUMAN ORGANIZATION* AS THE *MIND* MIRRORS REALITY!

DOES HUMANISM MAKE MY BUTT LOOK BIG?

RAISED ROMAN CATHOLIC, COMTE STOLE THE CHURCH'S ORGANIZATION WHOLESALE FOR WHAT HE CALLED HIS "RELIGION OF HUMANITY."

MY TURN!

HIS CHURCH WOULD BE OVERSEEN BY A POPE--ER, HIGH PRIEST (AND HE WOULD BE THE *FIRST*, OF COURSE).

COMTE RETAINED THE CATHOLIC *CALENDAR OF SAINTS*...BUT REPLACED MARTYRS WITH *SCIENTISTS!*

HAPPY *NEWTONMAS*, KIDS!

INSTEAD OF GETTING BAPTIZED, KIDS GET *"PRESENTED"* ... INSTEAD OF BEING CONFIRMED, TEENS GET *"INITIATED"*...

IT'S SO MUCH MORE *SCIENTIFIC* ... AND THEREFORE *AWESOME!*

(YOU GET THE IDEA.)

COMTE COINED THE TERM *"ALTRUISM,"* THE MORAL OBLIGATION TO SERVE *OTHERS*, TO DISTINGUISH HIS MOVEMENT FROM THE ENLIGHTENMENT'S INTEREST IN *"INDIVIDUAL RIGHTS,"* WHICH, IN HIS VIEW, WERE SELFISH AND *UNETHICAL!*

THERE BUT FOR THE GRACE OF *ME* GO I!

PLEASE HELP

WHEN LITTLE-H HUMANITY BEGINS *WORSHIPPING* BIG-H HUMANITY, COMTE BELIEVED ALTRUISM WOULD BE THE *RULE* TO HUMAN AFFAIRS, NOT THE EXCEPTION!

THE STATE AND RELIGION WOULD BE FUSED *TOGETHER*, JUST AS IN THE MIDDLE AGES, WITH *SCIENCE* PROVIDING ECONOMIC STRENGTH, AND PHILOSOPHY PROVIDING *MORAL AUTHORITY!*

"LOVE, THEN, IS OUR PRINCIPLE; ORDER OUR BASIS; AND PROGRESS OUR END!"

BRIGHT MAKES *RIGHT!*

GOOD LUCK WITH THAT, AUGUSTE!

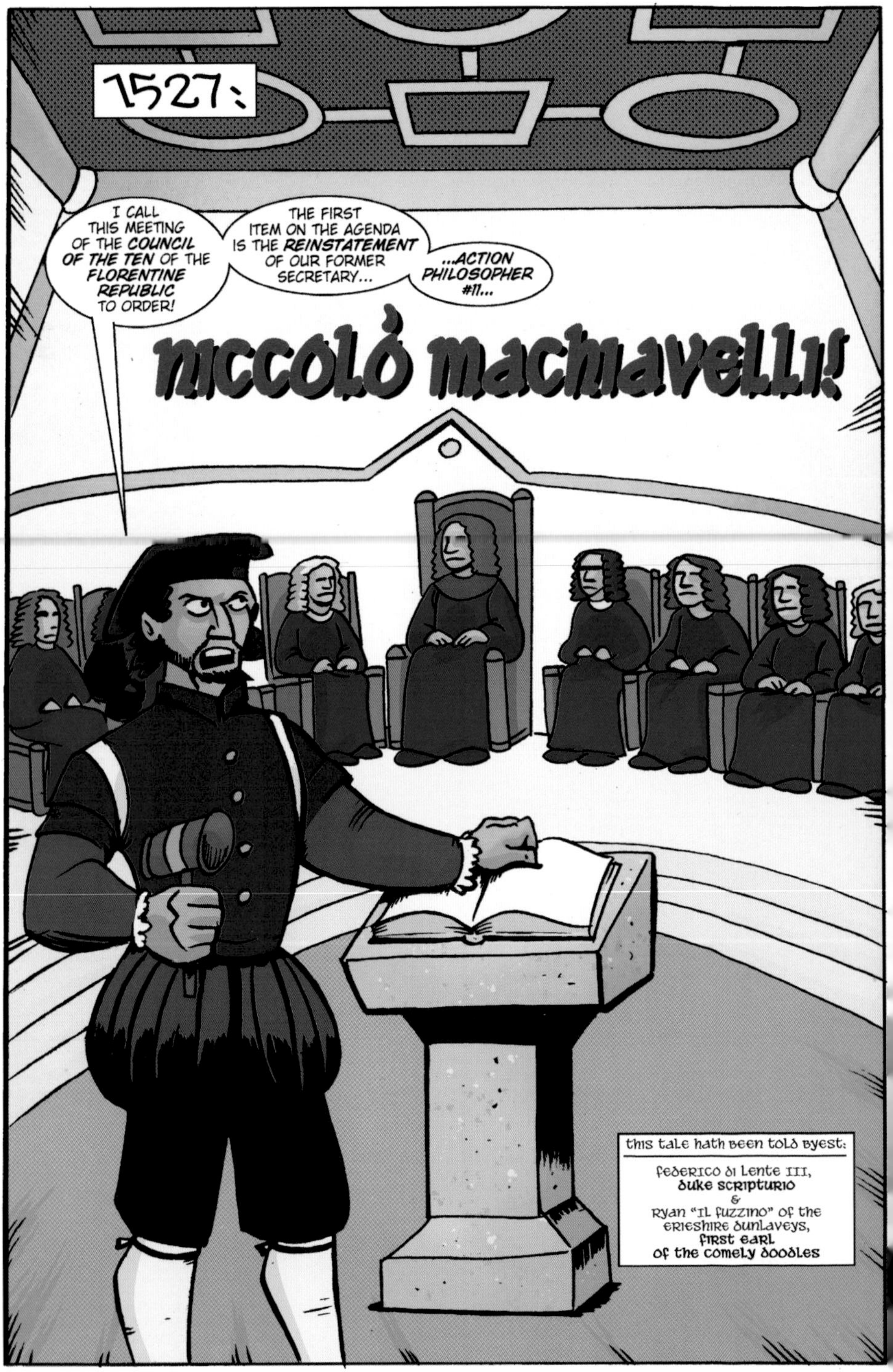
1527:
I CALL THIS MEETING OF THE COUNCIL OF THE TEN OF THE FLORENTINE REPUBLIC TO ORDER!
THE FIRST ITEM ON THE AGENDA IS THE REINSTATEMENT OF OUR FORMER SECRETARY...
...ACTION PHILOSOPHER #11...
NICCOLÒ MACHIAVELLI!
this tale hath been told byest:
federico di Lente III, duke scripturio & Ryan "Il fuzzino" of the erieshire dunlaveys, first earl of the comely doodles

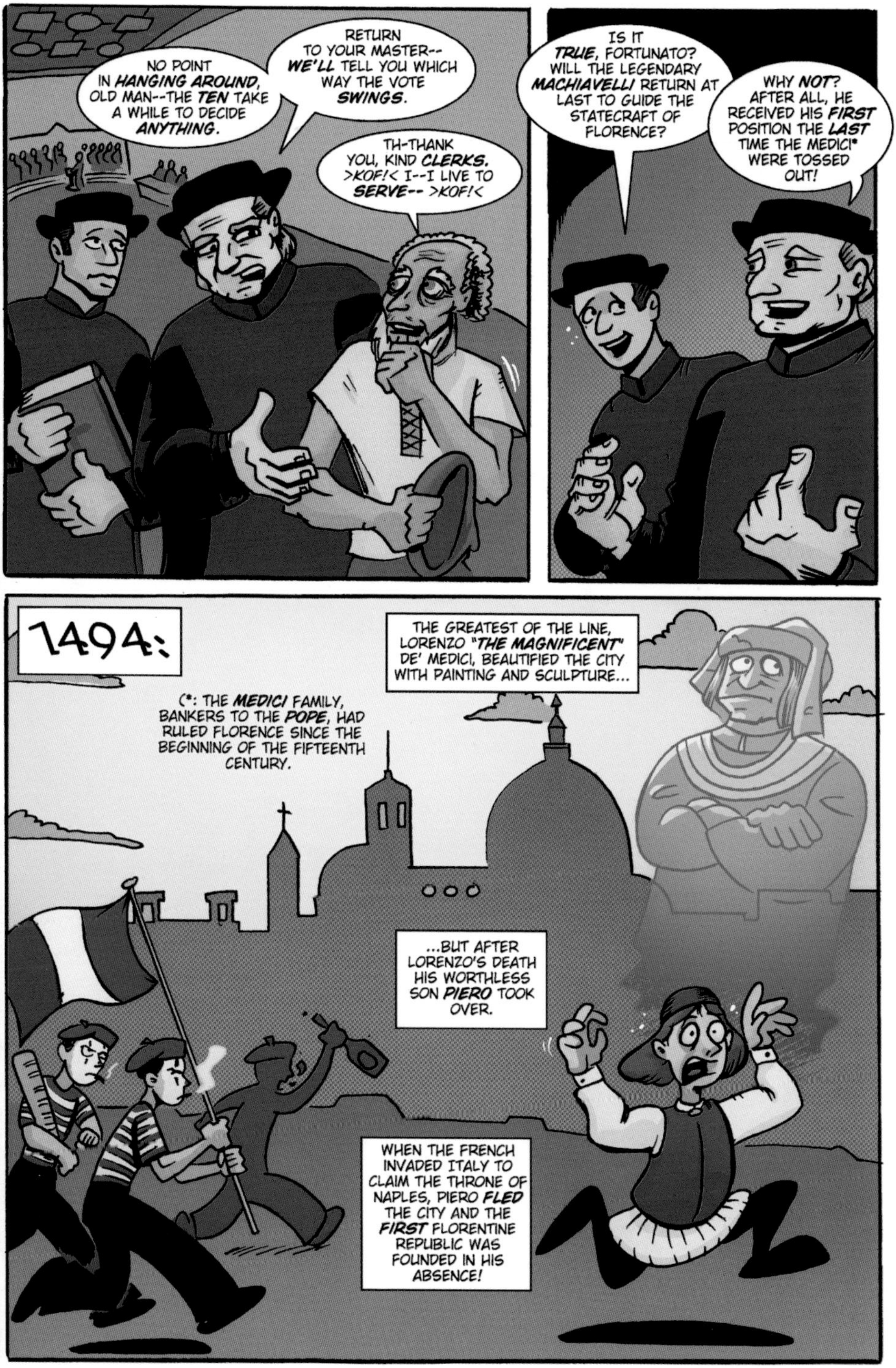
NO POINT IN HANGING AROUND, OLD MAN--THE TEN TAKE A WHILE TO DECIDE ANYTHING.
RETURN TO YOUR MASTER--WE'LL TELL YOU WHICH WAY THE VOTE SWINGS.
TH-THANK YOU, KIND CLERKS. >KOF!< I--I LIVE TO SERVE-- >KOF!<
IS IT TRUE, FORTUNATO? WILL THE LEGENDARY MACHIAVELLI RETURN AT LAST TO GUIDE THE STATECRAFT OF FLORENCE?
WHY NOT? AFTER ALL, HE RECEIVED HIS FIRST POSITION THE LAST TIME THE MEDICI* WERE TOSSED OUT!
1494:
THE GREATEST OF THE LINE, LORENZO "THE MAGNIFICENT" DE' MEDICI, BEAUTIFIED THE CITY WITH PAINTING AND SCULPTURE...
(*: THE MEDICI FAMILY, BANKERS TO THE POPE, HAD RULED FLORENCE SINCE THE BEGINNING OF THE FIFTEENTH CENTURY.
...BUT AFTER LORENZO'S DEATH HIS WORTHLESS SON PIERO TOOK OVER.
WHEN THE FRENCH INVADED ITALY TO CLAIM THE THRONE OF NAPLES, PIERO FLED THE CITY AND THE FIRST FLORENTINE REPUBLIC WAS FOUNDED IN HIS ABSENCE!

PIERO LATER ALLIED HIMSELF *WITH* THE FRENCH IN A BID TO REGAIN POWER, BUT HE *DROWNED* FLEEING A LOSING BATTLE, THUS EARNING HIM THE NICKNAME *"THE UNFORTUNATE"*...

GLUB!

DUMBASS

~~The WHIZZER~~

~~SCHMUCKBOY~~

~~SIR RUNS-A-LOT~~

The Unforunate

...THOUGH *OTHERS* WERE CONSIDERED.)

YOU'RE TOO *YOUNG* TO REMEMBER, MONTRESSOR, BUT THE EARLY DAYS OF THAT *FIRST* REPUBLIC WERE *DARK* INDEED!

"THE PEOPLE FELL UNDER THE SPELL OF *GIROLAMO SAVONAROLA* -- THE CRAZED PRIEST WHO PREACHED THAT THE SPLENDOR OF LORENZO'S *RENAISSANCE* WAS AN *AFFRONT* TO GOD!"

"HE ORDERED MIRRORS--COSMETICS--BOOKS--MUSICAL INSTRUMENTS--CAST ONTO HIS *BONFIRE OF THE VANITIES!*"

"HE ORDERED BOTICELLI TO THROW HIS *OWN* PAINTINGS INTO THE FLAMES!"

"WE TIRED OF HIS *ZEALOTRY* SOON ENOUGH, THOUGH. AFTER THE POPE *EXCOMMUNICATED* HIM WE *HANGED* AND *BURNED* HIM AT THE SAME TIME!"

"RIGHT...THAT'S OUR *EXTRA DOUBLE DELUXE* EXECUTION WITH CHEESE. I HEARD THAT MACHIAVELLI WAS *THERE!*"

it must be considered that there is nothing more difficult to carry out, nor more doubtful of success, nor more dangerous to handle, than to initiate a new order of things.

"I SUPPOSE IT'S *POSSIBLE*. NOT LONG *AFTER*, HE WAS APPOINTED SECRETARY TO THE REPUBLIC'S *SECOND CHANCERY*. HIS FIRST DIPLOMATIC MISSION WAS TO THE PROVINCE OF *ROMAGNA*, WHERE FRANCE'S ALLIES BESEIGED MILAN'S RULING *SFORZA* FAMILY. THOUGH THE SFORZAS' CASTLE WAS *IMPENETRABLE*, IT WAS OVERTHROWN FROM *WITHIN*. THE PEASANTS, SICK OF *OPPRESSION*, SIDED WITH THE *FRANCOPHILES!*"

I WOULD BLAME ANY RULER WHO, TRUSTING IN *FORTRESSES*, RECKS LITTLE OF BEING *HATED* BY HER PEOPLE.

"AT *FORLI*, MACHIAVELLI MET CESARE BORGIA, *DUKE VALENTINO*, WHO *LED* THE SEIGE."

"IS IT TRUE THAT MANY OF THE PAINTINGS OF *JESUS CHRIST* FROM THAT ERA WERE *BASED* ON THE HANDSOME DUKE, FORTUNATO?"

"WHY NOT? HE *WAS* THE SON OF POPE *ALEXANDER VI* AND ONE OF HIS MANY *MISTRESSES*, AFTER ALL. VALENTINO OWED *EVERYTHING* HE HAD TO HIS FATHER'S PATRONAGE OF FRANCE!"

ITALIA

JUST BRING IT HOME IN ONE *PIECE*.

GOLLY! *THANKS*, DAD!

"SOON *ALL* OF ROMAGNA FELL TO THE DUKE'S ARMIES. HE APPOINTED THE CRUEL *REMIRRO DE ORCO* ITS RULER!"

IN TAKING A STATE A CONQUEROR MUST ARRANGE TO COMMIT *ALL* HIS CRUELTIES AT *ONCE*, SO AS NOT TO HAVE TO RECUR TO THEM EVERY DAY.

FOR *INJURIES* SHOULD BE DONE ALL TOGETHER, SO THAT BEING *LESS* TASTED, THEY WILL GIVE LESS *OFFENSE*.

this man (REMIRRO), in a short time, was highly successful in rendering the country orderly and united.

REMIRRO **TERRORIZES** POOR FARMERS AND **IMPRISONS** THE PEASANTRY FOR NO **GOOD CAUSE**, DUKE VALENTINO!

HMMM... YOU DON'T **SAY**... THAT'S **AWFUL**... ~TSK!~

whereupon the Duke, not deeming such excessive authority **expedient**, lest it become **hateful**, resolved to show that if any cruelty had taken place, it was not by **his orders**, but through the harsh discipline of his **minister**.

Duke's Orders: Terrorize Imprison

there are many who think therefore that a wise prince ought, when he has the chance, to foment astutely some **enmity**, so that by **suppressing** it...

WHA-- WHAT I DO **WRONG?** ~GAK!~

...he will augment his **greatness.**

"WHO KNOWS HOW **FAR** VALENTINO COULD HAVE CLIMBED, HAD HIS **FATHER** NOT DIED SO SUDDENLY?"

"SCANDALMONGERS SAY THE POPE PLANNED TO POISON A **CARDINAL**, BUT THE WILY CLERIC SWITCHED THEIR SWEETMEAT BOXES, SO ALEXANDER'S OWN **TREACHERY** DID HIM IN!"

"**GOOD RIDDANCE**, I SAY. THE REPUBLIC SENT MACHIAVELLI TO **ROME** TO MONITOR THE ELECTION OF THE **NEW POPE**."

Go Pope!

"DUKE VALENTINO, SUFFERING FROM A **FEVER**, WAS MANIPULATED INTO ALLOWING AN ENEMY OF THE BORGIAS BE ELECTED **POPE JULIUS II!**"

"IF VALENTINO THOUGHT JULIUS WOULD BE **GRATEFUL**, HE WAS IN FOR A **NASTY** SURPRISE!"

whoever thinks that in high personages new benefits cause old offenses to be forgotten, makes a **great mistake.**

the Duke **erred** in his choice and it was the cause of his **ultimate ruin.**

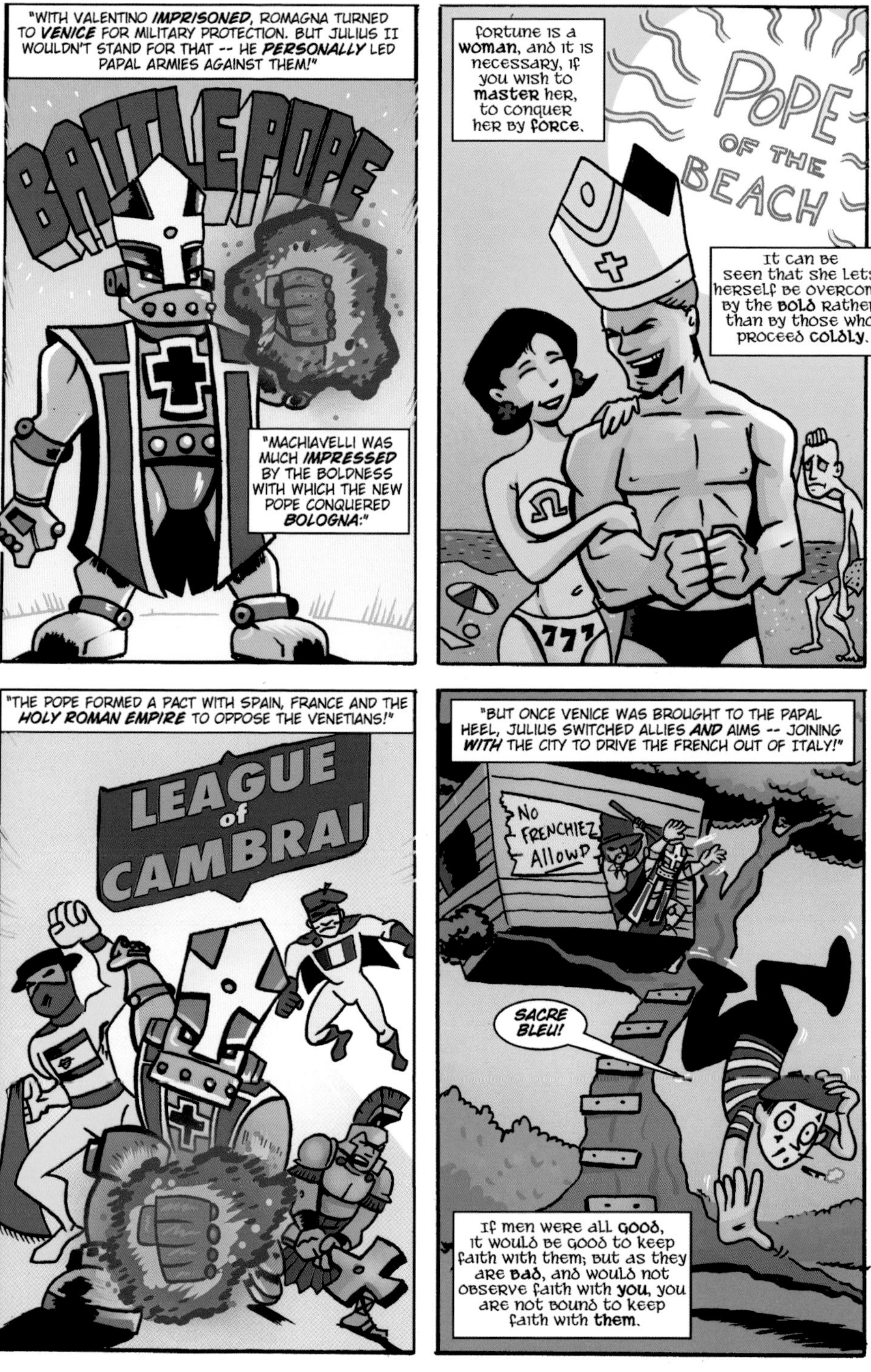
"WITH VALENTINO IMPRISONED, ROMAGNA TURNED TO VENICE FOR MILITARY PROTECTION. BUT JULIUS II WOULDN'T STAND FOR THAT -- HE PERSONALLY LED PAPAL ARMIES AGAINST THEM!"
BATTLE POPE
"MACHIAVELLI WAS MUCH IMPRESSED BY THE BOLDNESS WITH WHICH THE NEW POPE CONQUERED BOLOGNA:"
fortune is a woman, and it is necessary, if you wish to master her, to conquer her by force.
POPE OF THE BEACH
It can be seen that she lets herself be overcome by the bold rather than by those who proceed coldly.
Ω
777
"THE POPE FORMED A PACT WITH SPAIN, FRANCE AND THE HOLY ROMAN EMPIRE TO OPPOSE THE VENETIANS!"
LEAGUE of CAMBRAI
"BUT ONCE VENICE WAS BROUGHT TO THE PAPAL HEEL, JULIUS SWITCHED ALLIES AND AIMS -- JOINING WITH THE CITY TO DRIVE THE FRENCH OUT OF ITALY!"
No FRENCHIEZ Allowd
SACRE BLEU!
If men were all good, it would be good to keep faith with them; but as they are bad, and would not observe faith with you, you are not bound to keep faith with them.

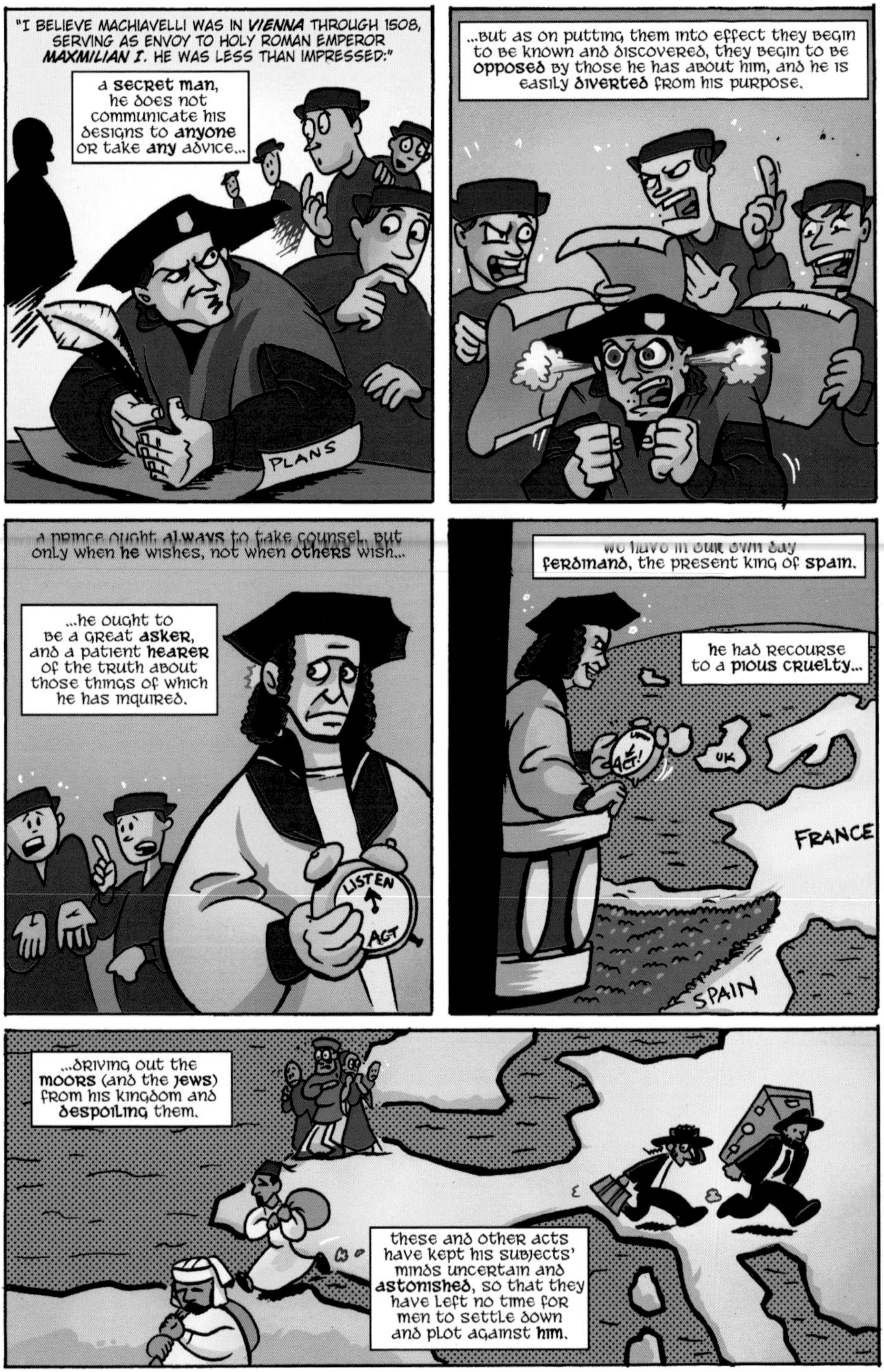
"I BELIEVE MACHIAVELLI WAS IN VIENNA THROUGH 1508, SERVING AS ENVOY TO HOLY ROMAN EMPEROR MAXMILIAN I. HE WAS LESS THAN IMPRESSED:"
a secret man, he does not communicate his designs to anyone or take any advice...
PLANS
...but as on putting them into effect they begin to be known and discovered, they begin to be opposed by those he has about him, and he is easily diverted from his purpose.
A prince ought always to take counsel, but only when he wishes, not when others wish...
...he ought to be a great asker, and a patient hearer of the truth about those things of which he has inquired.
LISTEN
ACT
we have in our own day ferdinand, the present king of spain.
he had recourse to a pious cruelty...
UK
FRANCE
SPAIN
...driving out the moors (and the jews) from his kingdom and despoiling them.
these and other acts have kept his subjects' minds uncertain and astonished, so that they have left no time for men to settle down and plot against him.

"IT TOOK ALL OF MACHIAVELLI AND HIS FELLOW MINISTERS' *DIPLOMATIC SKILLS* TO KEEP FLORENCE *OUT* OF THE ITALIAN WARS. BUT HE LEARNED THE *HARD WAY:*"

IRRESOLUTE PRINCES, TO AVOID *PRESENT* DANGERS, USUALLY FOLLOW THE WAY OF *NEUTRALITY*, AND ARE MOSTLY *RUINED* BY IT.

"THE POPE COULD NO LONGER RISK THE POSSIBILITY THAT FLORENCE MIGHT ALLY WITH HIS *ENEMIES.* IN 1512, FERDINAND'S ARMIES OCCUPIED THE CITY, AND THEN, BY *PAPAL DECREE...*"

HONEY, I'M *HOME!*

"...JULIUS II RETURNED THE *MEDICIS* TO POWER! *GIULIANO*, PIERO'S BROTHER, BECAME THE CITY'S NEW DUKE!"

"A MEDICI *GOON SQUAD* SOON ARRESTED TWO YOUNG REPUBLICAN *CONSPIRATORS* WITH A LIST OF PEOPLE THEY THOUGHT MIGHT BE *SYMPATHETIC* TO AN OVERTHROW OF PAPAL CONTROL!"

?

"GUESS WHO'S NAME THEY FOUND ON IT?"

PHILLIP BARADUCCI
CHARLES CIPPRIANO
NICCOLÒ MACHIAVELLI
WILLIAM PAGANO
ANTHONY MARANO

"~GASP!~ DID MACHIAVELLI *NAME NAMES?*"

"HOW *COULD* HE? HE HAD *NO IDEA* HOW HIS NAME GOT ON THE LIST IN THE *FIRST PLACE!*"

"HIS LIFE WAS **SPARED**-- BUT THE MEDICI BANISHED HIM TO A FARM IN THE **SUBURBS**, HIS GOVERNMENT POSITION FOREVER **LOST**!"

"-:**FEH**!:- SOME **MERCY**! TO EXILE ONE SUCH AS **NICCOLO** FROM THE HALLS OF POWER ... THEY MIGHT AS WELL HAVE CUT OFF HIS **AIR SUPPLY**!"

STILL, HE FOUND A WAY TO KEEP BUSY IN HIS **LIBRARY**:

ON THE THRESHOLD I SLIP OFF MY DAY'S CLOTHES WITH THEIR MUD AND DIRT, PUT ON MY CURIAL ROBES, AND ENTER THE ANCIENT COURTS OF THE MEN OF OLD.

I AM NOT ASHAMED TO ADDRESS THEM AND **ASK** THEM THE REASONS FOR THEIR ACTION, AND THEY **REPLY** CONSIDERATELY; AND FOR TWO HOURS I **FORGET** ALL MY CARES.

AND SINCE **DANTE** SAYS THAT WE CAN NEVER ATTAIN KNOWLEDGE UNLESS WE RETAIN WHAT WE HEAR, I HAVE NOTED DOWN THE CAPITAL I HAVE ACCUMULATED FROM THEIR CONVERSATION AND COMPOSED A LITTLE BOOK...

"HE DEDICATED HIS WORK TO PIERO'S SON **LORENZO** IN AN ATTEMPT TO WIN THE FAVOR OF THE MEDICIS AND RECLAIM HIS POSITION!"

"IT CONTAINED THE **SUM TOTAL** OF MACHIAVELLI'S STUDY OF ANCIENT LORE, COMBINED WITH HIS **DECADES** OF EXPERIENCE IN GOVERNMENT SERVICE!"

THE HEREIN-MENTIONED THINGS, IF **PRUDENTLY** OBSERVED, MAKE A **NEW PRINCE** SEEM **ANCIENT**, AND RENDER HIM AT ONCE MORE SECURE AND FIRMER IN THE STATE THAN IF HE HAD BEEN ESTABLISHED THERE OF OLD.

IL PRINCIPE

72

my intention being to write something of **use** to those who understand, it appears to me more proper to go to the real **truth** of the matter than to its imagination.

how we live is so far removed from how we **ought** to live, that he who abandons what **is** done for what **ought** to be done, will rather learn how to bring about his own **ruin** than his preservation.

a man who wishes to make a profession of **goodness** in **everything** must necessarily come to grief among so many who are **not** good.

therefore it is necessary for a **prince**, who wishes to **maintain** himself...

...to learn how **not** to be good.

everybody sees what you **appear** to be, and few feel what you **are**, and those few will not dare to oppose themselves to the **many**.

in the actions of men, and especially of **princes**, from which there is **no appeal**...

...the **end** justifies the **means**.

"THE STUPID BRAT NEVER *READ* THE COPY OF *THE PRINCE* MACHIAVELLI PRESENTED TO HIM--"

"--IF HE *HAD*, MAYBE HIS FAMILY WOULDN'T HAVE BEEN *EXILED* AGAIN!"

CHICK!

"THE PEOPLE OF FLORENCE TURNED AGAINST THE POPE WHEN FOREIGN TROOPS --HIS *OWN ALLIES*-- SACKED ROME!"

"WE *REPUBLICANS* ARE BACK ON *TOP* AGAIN!"

SINCE THEN, *THE PRINCE* HAS BECOME RENOWNED *ACROSS* EUROPE--EVEN *I* HAVE WHOLE *CHAPTERS* MEMORIZED!

WITH *MACHIAVELLI* AGAIN AT THE HELM OF FLORENCE'S STATE-CRAFT, NO DOUBT THE REPUBLIC'S SECURITY IS *ASSURED*--

SSSHH!! SOUNDS LIKE DEBATE IS *WINDING DOWN*--

SO IT'S *UNANIMOUS* THEN!

THANKS TO OUR FORMER SECRETARY'S *CYNICAL SCREED*, THE VERY WORD *"MACHIAVELLIAN"* HAS BECOME A SYNONYM FOR *RUTHLESS DUPLICITY!*

WE CANNOT HAVE SUCH A PERSON WORKING FOR *US!*

THE CITIZENS OF FLORENCE MUST KNOW THEIR GOVERNMENT IS RULED BY *FAITH, CHARITY* AND *RELIGION!*

SIGNOR MACHIAVELLI'S PETITION IS *REJECTED!*

BU-BUT... MACHIAVELLI DID NOTHING MORE THAN TELL THE *TRUTH* ABOUT HOW POWER WAS WIELDED IN HIS TIMES--

EXACTLY! ONE OF THE *WORST* THINGS YOU CAN DO IN GOVERNMENT IS BE *SMARTER* THAN YOUR SUPERIORS!

HE FORGOT ONE OF HIS *OWN* MAXIMS--

IT IS NOT, THEREFORE, NECESSARY FOR A PRINCE TO HAVE FAITH, CHARITY AND RELIGION...

THE *NEXT* BILL WOULD ALLOW US TO DEDUCT OUR *MISTRESSES* AS *BUSINESS EXPENSES!* ALL THOSE IN FAVOR--?

AYE!

AYE!

AYE!

AYE!

...BUT IT IS NECESSARY TO *SEEM* TO HAVE THEM.

GUESS WE'D BETTER FIND THAT *SERVANT* SO HE CAN GIVE HIS MASTER THE *BAD NEWS*...

UH-OH! SEE WHERE ALL THOSE *PEOPLE* ARE GATHERED--ISN'T THAT THE ADDRESS HE *GAVE* US?

WHAT HAS *HAPPENED*, SIGNORA?

>SOB!< POOR SIGNOR *MACHIAVELLI*--THE FEVER *FELLED* HIM AS SOON AS HE GOT BACK FROM THE PALAZZO VECCHIO!

I DIDN'T EVEN *RECOGNIZE* HIM -- THE TORTURE HAS *AGED* HIM SO, THE POOR PAPER-PUSHER!

GASP! THAT BROKEN-DOWN OLD *FARMER*... *HE* WAS THE FEARED MACHIAVELLI?!

MACHIAVELLI DIED WITHOUT EVER LEARNING THAT HIS BELOVED FLORENTINE REPUBLIC HAD *OVERWHELMINGLY REFUSED* TO RETURN HIM TO OFFICE.

AND "*HONEST MEN*" HAVE USED HIS NAME AS A *PEJORATIVE* EVER SINCE!

IL FINITO

75

THOMAS HOBBES

(1588-1679) WAS WORKING AS A *TUTOR* IN *PARIS* WHEN THE ENGLISH CIVIL WAR BROKE OUT.

TIME SPENT WITH EXILED BRITISH *ROYALS* AND THEIR *SYMPATHIZERS* IN FRANCE INSPIRED HOBBES TO WRITE HIS LANDMARK WORK OF *POLITICAL* PHILOSOPHY, *LEVIATHAN, OR THE MATTER, FORM AND POWER OF A COMMONWEALTH, ECCLESIASTICAL AND CIVIL* (1650).

THE TITLE INVOKES THE GIANT BIBLICAL *SEA MONSTER*, TO WHICH HOBBES COMPARES THE STATE -- A GREAT BEAST, IN ESSENCE, COMPRISED OF *MEN*.

WITHOUT CIVIL SOCIETY, HOBBES WARNS, HUMANITY WOULD FALL INTO *BELLUM OMNIUM CONTRA OMNES* -- "WAR OF ALL *AGAINST* ALL."

EACH CITIZEN SAYS, IN EFFECT, TO THE SOVEREIGN:

I AUTHORIZE AND *GIVE UP* MY RIGHT OF GOVERNING *MYSELF* TO *THIS* MAN ON THE CONDITION THAT MY *FELLOW* CITIZENS GIVE UP *THEIR* RIGHT TO HIM, AND AUTHORIZE ALL HIS ACTIONS IN *LIKE* MANNER.

TO THE SOVEREIGN HOBBES GIVES NEARLY *UNFETTERED* POWER TO MAINTAIN THE PEACE, INCLUDING SUPERSEDING THE COURTS, USING *CENSORSHIP* TO SQUASH "DISRUPTIVE" SPEECH, AND THE SOLE RIGHT TO NAME HIS *SUCCESSOR*.

HE CANNOT BE HELD ACCOUNTABLE BY HIS OWN *SUBJECTS*, WHO HAVE NO JEFFERSONIAN *"RIGHT TO REBELLION"*, FOR OVERTHROWING THE SOVEREIGN WOULD RETURN PEOPLE TO THE AFOREMENTIONED *REALLY BAD* STATE OF NATURE.

NEVERTHELESS, EXCEPT FOR THOSE CONSTRAINTS ABSOLUTELY *NECESSARY* TO MAINTAIN THE PEACE, THE SOVEREIGN SHOULD ALLOW FOR HIS SUBJECTS' MAXIMUM *INDEPENDENCE*, HOBBES SAYS.

IN THIS WOEFUL "STATE OF *NATURE*", "EVERY MAN HAS A RIGHT TO *EVERY* THING, EVEN TO ONE ANOTHER'S *BODY*"-- WHICH WOULD MAKE A MAN'S LIFE "SOLITARY, POOR, NASTY, BRUTISH, AND *SHORT*."

TO OBTAIN *SECURITY* AGAINST CONSTANT VIOLENCE TO ONE'S PERSON, EACH MAN AGREES TO A *SOCIAL CONTRACT* ... HE *GIVES UP* THE IMMEDIATE GRATIFICATION OF ALL HIS *DESIRES* (WHICH BRING HIM INTO CONFLICT AND WITH OTHER MEN, THUS *SPARKING* VIOLENCE).

AND TO THE *STATE* HE GIVES A *MONOPOLY* ON THE JUST USE OF *FORCE*.

NEIGHBOR HOOD WATCH

KING of the SUBURBS

...AND WHEN *ANOTHER* STATE VIOLATES AGREE-MENTS WITH *OUR* STATE, THE *ARMY* IS ALLOWED TO USE VIOLENCE AGAINST *IT*.

POLICE ARE ALLOWED TO USE VIOLENCE TO KEEP THE PEACE AMONG *CITIZENS*...

"A GATED COMMUNITY"

UNFORTUNATELY, AS THERE IS NO APPEAL TO AN EARTHLY POWER *HIGHER* THAN THE SOVEREIGN, CITIZENS ARE ENTIRELY DEPENDANT ON THE SOVEREIGN'S OWN *GOODNESS* (OR LACK THEREOF) FOR HIM TO ADHERE TO THIS PRINCIPLE.

IRONICALLY, HOBBES' ROYALIST BUDDIES *DESPISED* LEVIATHAN BECAUSE THEY THOUGHT IT WAS EXCESSIVELY *SECULAR*. AFTER THEY THREATENED HIS *LIFE* HE HAD TO FLEE TO ENGLAND AND PETITION THE REBEL *CROMWELLIANS* FOR SANCTUARY!

THERE'S A SWISS WHO JUST CAN'T MISS WHEN YOUR BRAIN'S AMISS AND YOU HATE YOUR SIS...

OH NO, ROUSSEAU!

"OH NO, ROUSSEAU" WAS FILMED BEFORE A *LIVE STUDIO AUDIENCE.*

MADAM LEVASSEUR! I'M HOME!

WHOOOO!! CLAP CLAP CLAP!!

MADAM LEVASSEUR?

I'VE RETURNED FROM LEAVING OUR *FIFTH* ILLEGITIMATE CHILD AT THE *FOUNDLINGS' HOSPITAL!*

POOR LITTLE ONES... "MAN IS *BORN FREE;* AND EVERYWHERE HE IS IN *CHAINS!"**

HA! HA! HA! HA! HA!

*: J.J.R., ON THE SOCIAL CONTRACT (1762)

WHERE *IS* THAT BLASTED *MISTRESS*-SLASH-*HOUSEKEEPER* OF MINE?

EH? WHAT IS IT, SULTAN? IS THERE SOMETHING IN THERE YOU WANT ME TO *SEE,* BOY?

arf! arf!

scritch scritch

AH! *THERE* YOU ARE!

OOOOOOHHH...

MONSIEUR ROUSSEAU!

YOU'RE BACK FROM THE ORPHANAGE *ALREADY*? THAT WAS *QUICK!*

I GOT IN THE *"TEN FOUNDLINGS OR LESS"* LINE!

IS THAT-- FAMED SCOTTISH BIOGRAPHER *JAMES BOSWELL?* I WASN'T EXPECTING YOU TO COME UNTIL *NEXT WEEK!*

HA! HA!

I WAS STARTING TO THINK HE WASN'T GOING TO COME AT *ALL...*

OOOOOOHHH... HA! HA!

MONSIEUR-- PLEASE-- I *SWEAR*--THIS *ISN'T* WHAT IT LOOKS LIKE!

ACTUALLY, MY DEAR BOSWELL, I AM *MORE* CONCERNED WITH WHAT IT *DOESN'T* LOOK LIKE!

IT *DOESN'T* LOOK LIKE MADAM LE VASSEUR IS FIXING ME A *HOT COCOA* WHILE I *MASTURBATE!*

-UGH!- *T.M.I.,* J.J.!

NONSENSE! "I PROPOSE TO SHOW MY FELLOWS A MAN AS *NATURE* MADE HIM"...

"...AND THIS MAN IS *MYSELF!"**

HA! HA! HA!

**: J.J.R., CONFESSIONS (1782)

78

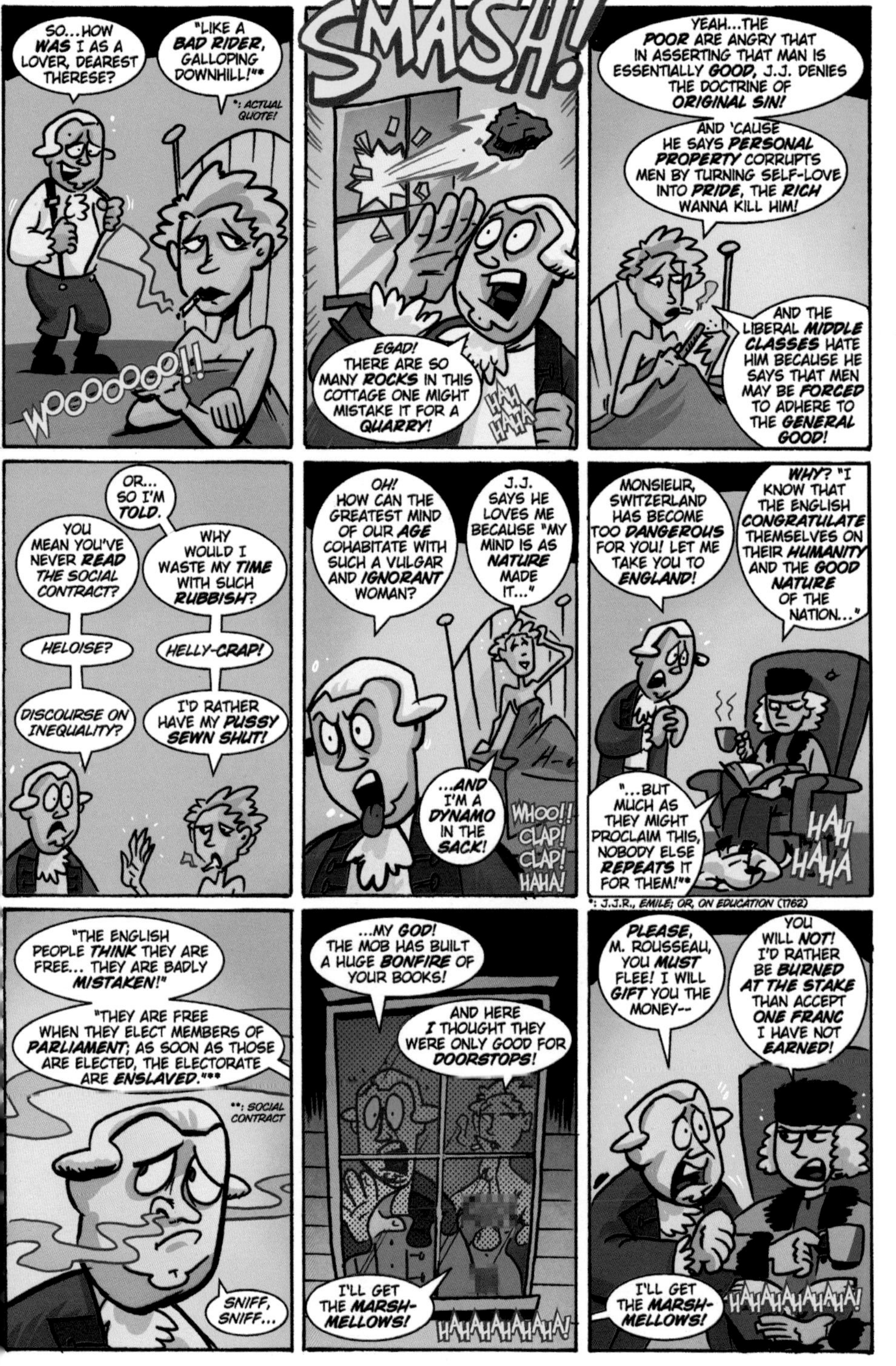
SO...HOW WAS I AS A LOVER, DEAREST THERESE?
"LIKE A BAD RIDER, GALLOPING DOWNHILL!"*
*: ACTUAL QUOTE!
WOOOOOOOO!!!
SMASH!
EGAD! THERE ARE SO MANY ROCKS IN THIS COTTAGE ONE MIGHT MISTAKE IT FOR A QUARRY!
HAH HAHA
YEAH...THE POOR ARE ANGRY THAT IN ASSERTING THAT MAN IS ESSENTIALLY GOOD, J.J. DENIES THE DOCTRINE OF ORIGINAL SIN!
AND 'CAUSE HE SAYS PERSONAL PROPERTY CORRUPTS MEN BY TURNING SELF-LOVE INTO PRIDE, THE RICH WANNA KILL HIM!
AND THE LIBERAL MIDDLE CLASSES HATE HIM BECAUSE HE SAYS THAT MEN MAY BE FORCED TO ADHERE TO THE GENERAL GOOD!
OR... SO I'M TOLD.
YOU MEAN YOU'VE NEVER READ THE SOCIAL CONTRACT?
WHY WOULD I WASTE MY TIME WITH SUCH RUBBISH?
HELOISE?
HELLY-CRAP!
DISCOURSE ON INEQUALITY?
I'D RATHER HAVE MY PUSSY SEWN SHUT!
OH! HOW CAN THE GREATEST MIND OF OUR AGE COHABITATE WITH SUCH A VULGAR AND IGNORANT WOMAN?
J.J. SAYS HE LOVES ME BECAUSE "MY MIND IS AS NATURE MADE IT..."
...AND I'M A DYNAMO IN THE SACK!
WHOO!! CLAP! CLAP! HAHA!
MONSIEUR, SWITZERLAND HAS BECOME TOO DANGEROUS FOR YOU! LET ME TAKE YOU TO ENGLAND!
WHY? "I KNOW THAT THE ENGLISH CONGRATULATE THEMSELVES ON THEIR HUMANITY AND THE GOOD NATURE OF THE NATION..."
"...BUT MUCH AS THEY MIGHT PROCLAIM THIS, NOBODY ELSE REPEATS IT FOR THEM!"*
HAH HAHA
*: J.J.R., EMILE; OR, ON EDUCATION (1762)
"THE ENGLISH PEOPLE THINK THEY ARE FREE... THEY ARE BADLY MISTAKEN!"
"THEY ARE FREE WHEN THEY ELECT MEMBERS OF PARLIAMENT; AS SOON AS THOSE ARE ELECTED, THE ELECTORATE ARE ENSLAVED."**
**: SOCIAL CONTRACT
SNIFF, SNIFF...
...MY GOD! THE MOB HAS BUILT A HUGE BONFIRE OF YOUR BOOKS!
AND HERE I THOUGHT THEY WERE ONLY GOOD FOR DOORSTOPS!
I'LL GET THE MARSH-MELLOWS!
HAHAHAHAHAHA!
PLEASE, M. ROUSSEAU, YOU MUST FLEE! I WILL GIFT YOU THE MONEY--
YOU WILL NOT! I'D RATHER BE BURNED AT THE STAKE THAN ACCEPT ONE FRANC I HAVE NOT EARNED!
I'LL GET THE MARSH-MELLOWS!
HAHAHAHAHAHA!

BUT *THINK* ABOUT ALL YOUR WRITINGS STILL HAVE TO OFFER *MANKIND*--

"MANKIND *DISGUSTS* ME! MY HOUSEKEEPER TELLS ME THAT I AM IN *FAR* BETTER HUMOR ON THE DAYS WHEN I'VE BEEN *ALONE!*"

I *ALSO* SAID I'D BE IN FAR BETTER HUMOR ON THE DAY HE WAS *DEAD!*

HA!

ALONE, EH?

THAT GIVES ME AN *IDEA...*

...AND IT'S SO *CRAZY* IT MIGHT *JUST WORK...*

HAHA WOOOO! CLAP! CLAP! CLAP!

"OH NO, ROUSSEAU" WILL BE RIGHT *BACK,* AFTER *THESE* MESSAGES...

OH NO, *Rousseau!*

"THE FIRST MAN WHO, HAVING *FENCED IN* A PIECE OF LAND, SAID;"

"THIS IS MINE!"

"AND FOUND PEOPLE NAIVE ENOUGH TO *BELIEVE* HIM... *THAT* MAN WAS THE TRUE *FOUNDER OF CIVIL SOCIETY!*"*

*: J.J.R., DISCOURSE ON THE ORIGIN AND BASIS OF INEQUALITY AMONG MEN (1754)

OG: FOUNDER OF CIVIL SOCIETY

THURSDAYS 8pm ET

STAY *BACK,* YOU RABBLE!

I JUST WANT TO BE *ALONE!* ~GROAN!~

THERESE! I'VE RETURNED FROM HANDING OUT *RIBBONS* TO THE VILLAGE GIRLS TO REMIND THEM TO *BREAST-FEED* THEIR BABIES!

HA! HA! HA!

IT *IS* NATURE'S WAY, AFTER ALL...

Rousseau? HELL NO!

JEAN-JACQUES ROUSSEAU!!

MON DIEU! WHO --OR *WHAT*-- ARE YOU?!

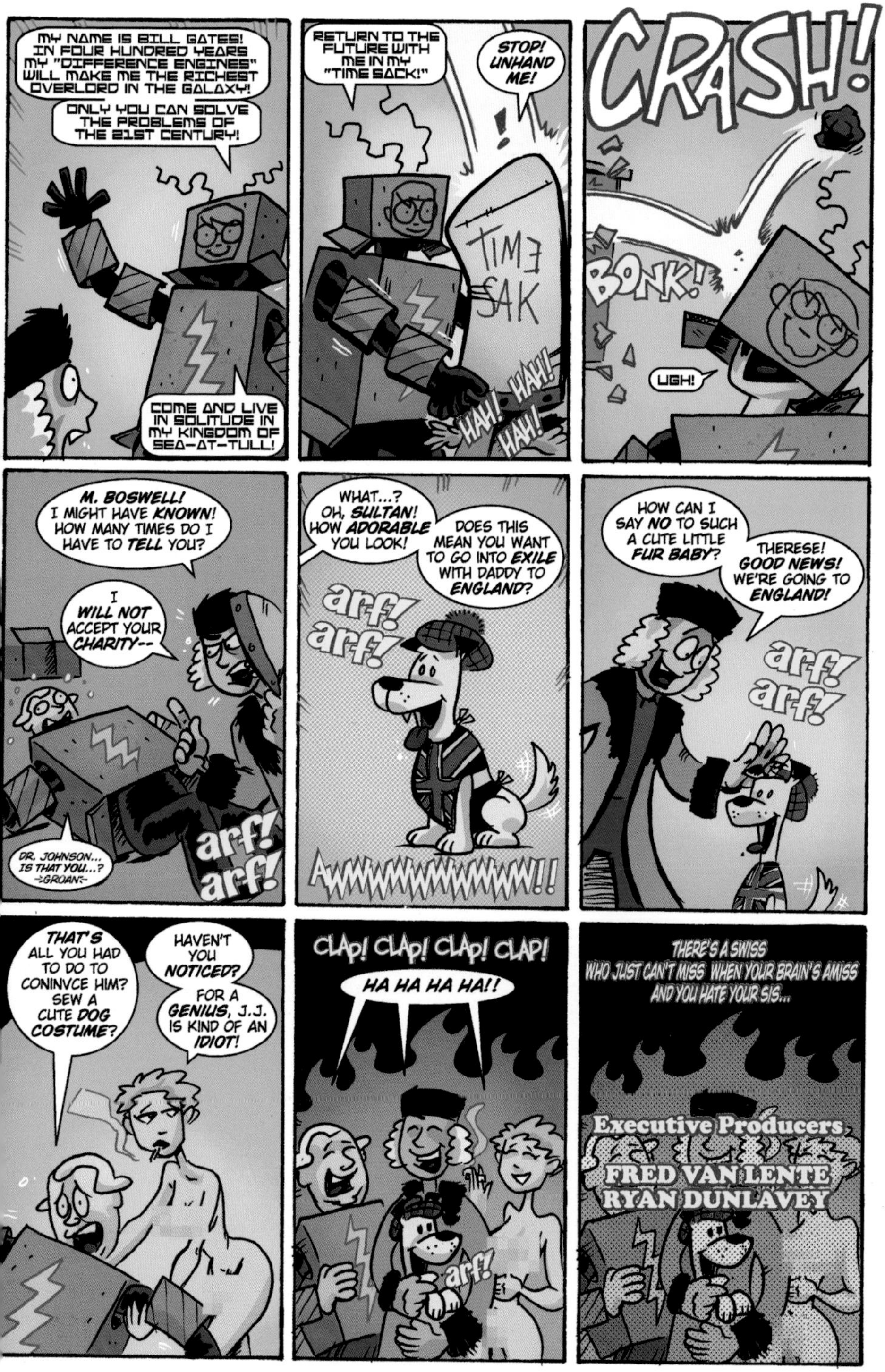
MY NAME IS BILL GATES! IN FOUR HUNDRED YEARS MY "DIFFERENCE ENGINES" WILL MAKE ME THE RICHEST OVERLORD IN THE GALAXY!
ONLY YOU CAN SOLVE THE PROBLEMS OF THE 21ST CENTURY!
COME AND LIVE IN SOLITUDE IN MY KINGDOM OF SEA-AT-TULL!
RETURN TO THE FUTURE WITH ME IN MY "TIME SACK!"
STOP! UNHAND ME!
TIME SAK
HAH! HAH! HAH! HAH!
CRASH!
BONK!
UGH!
M. BOSWELL! I MIGHT HAVE KNOWN! HOW MANY TIMES DO I HAVE TO TELL YOU?
I WILL NOT ACCEPT YOUR CHARITY--
DR. JOHNSON... IS THAT YOU...? ~GROAN~
arf! arf!
WHAT...? OH, SULTAN! HOW ADORABLE YOU LOOK!
DOES THIS MEAN YOU WANT TO GO INTO EXILE WITH DADDY TO ENGLAND?
arf! arf!
AWWWWWWWWWWW!!
HOW CAN I SAY NO TO SUCH A CUTE LITTLE FUR BABY?
THERESE! GOOD NEWS! WE'RE GOING TO ENGLAND!
arf! arf!
THAT'S ALL YOU HAD TO DO TO CONINVCE HIM? SEW A CUTE DOG COSTUME?
HAVEN'T YOU NOTICED?
FOR A GENIUS, J.J. IS KIND OF AN IDIOT!
CLAP! CLAP! CLAP! CLAP!
HA HA HA HA!!
arf!
THERE'S A SWISS WHO JUST CAN'T MISS WHEN YOUR BRAIN'S AMISS AND YOU HATE YOUR SIS...
Executive Producers
FRED VAN LENTE
RYAN DUNLAVEY

IN JUNE, 1776, THE **CONTINENTAL CONGRESS** OF THE REBELLIOUS THIRTEEN AMERICAN COLONIES COULD AGREE ON ALMOST **NOTHING** -- EXCEPT THE NEED TO **ARTICULATE** THEIR GRIEVANCES WITH THE **BRITISH CROWN!**

THE MAN DRAFTED TO **DRAFT** THIS **DECLARATION** WAS THE **QUIETEST** DELEGATE IN CONGRESS--A MAN WHOSE OWN **SPEAKING VOICE** BARELY ROSE ABOVE A **WHISPER**--BUT WAS **UNANIMOUSLY AGREED** TO BE THE GREATEST **POLITICAL WRITER** IN THE COUNTRY...

...A MAN **WE** KNOW BETTER AS **ACTION PHILOSOPHER #4:**

Thomas Jefferson!

We mutually pledge to each other our lives, our fortunes and our sacred honor.
Frederick J. Van Lente (script)
Ryan Michael Dunlavey (art)

JEFFERSON AUTHORED WHAT TURNED OUT TO BE **AMERICAN SCRIPTURE**, BUT IT WAS THE **CROWNING ACHIEVEMENT** OF **THE ENLIGHTENMENT**, ITSELF A **REVOLUTIONARY** SHIFT IN EUROPEAN PHILOSOPHY!

IN CONGRESS, JULY 4, 1776.
The unanimous Declaration of the ~~~~ States of America.

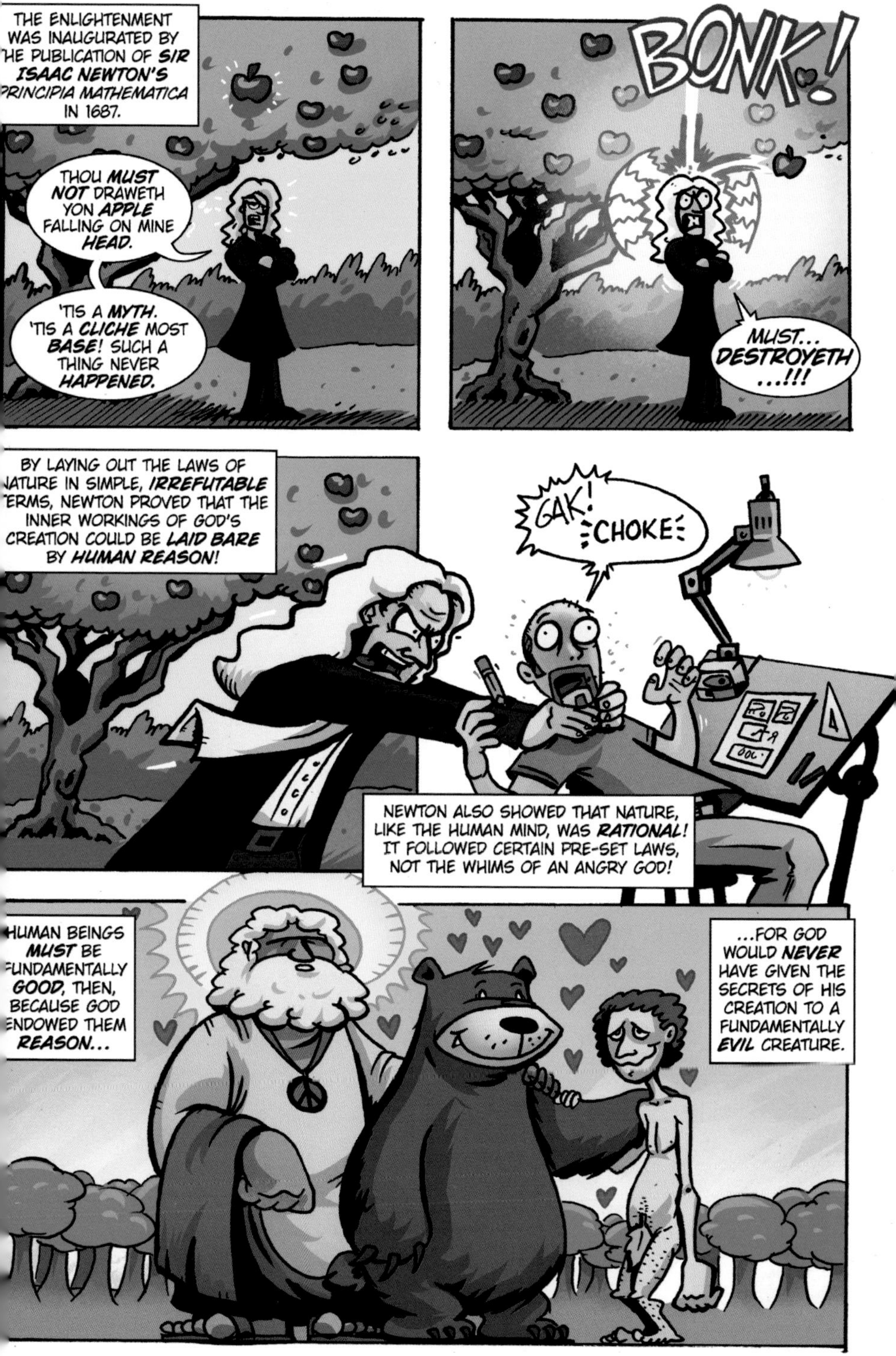

THE ENLIGHTENMENT WAS INAUGURATED BY HE PUBLICATION OF SIR ISAAC NEWTON'S RINCIPIA MATHEMATICA IN 1687.
THOU MUST NOT DRAWETH YON APPLE FALLING ON MINE HEAD.
'TIS A MYTH. 'TIS A CLICHE MOST BASE! SUCH A THING NEVER HAPPENED.
BONK!
MUST... DESTROYETH ...!!!
BY LAYING OUT THE LAWS OF ATURE IN SIMPLE, IRREFUTABLE ERMS, NEWTON PROVED THAT THE INNER WORKINGS OF GOD'S CREATION COULD BE LAID BARE BY HUMAN REASON!
GAK! CHOKE
NEWTON ALSO SHOWED THAT NATURE, LIKE THE HUMAN MIND, WAS RATIONAL! IT FOLLOWED CERTAIN PRE-SET LAWS, NOT THE WHIMS OF AN ANGRY GOD!
HUMAN BEINGS MUST BE FUNDAMENTALLY GOOD, THEN, BECAUSE GOD ENDOWED THEM REASON...
...FOR GOD WOULD NEVER HAVE GIVEN THE SECRETS OF HIS CREATION TO A FUNDAMENTALLY EVIL CREATURE.

UNLESS, OF COURSE, YOU PREFER THE *"GOD IS A TOTAL RETARD"* THEORY.

MANY CRITICS DERIDED THE ENLIGHTENMENT THINKERS AS HOPELESSLY *NAIVE.* AFTER ALL, THIS WAS A *RADICAL DEVIATION* FROM *CENTURIES* OF CHRISTIAN THOUGHT!

THROUGHOUT THE *MIDDLE AGES* IT WAS PRESUMED THAT HUMANS WERE HOPELESSLY *CORRUPT.* OUR EXPULSION FROM EDEN *ALIENATED* US FROM GOD AND WE WOULD ACHIEVE UNION WITH HIM ONLY IN *DEATH!*

TO ENLIGHTENMENT THINKERS, HOWEVER, THIS ALIENATION WAS THE RESULT OF AN OVERLY COMPLICATED, *MANMADE* ECCLESIASTICAL BUREAUCRACY THAT HAD NO *COUNTERPART* IN NATURE!

I'M *SORRY*, SIR, HE'S *VERY* BUSY, SO IF YOU DON'T HAVE AN *APPOINTMENT* I'M AFRAID I CAN'T LET YOU IN...

GOD

Z

ONLY BY DOING *AWAY* WITH MANMADE *CONSTRUCTS* AND CLEAVING CLOSE TO OUR *OWN* INNATE *NATURE* COULD WE BE TRULY GOOD, INNOCENT, AND (THEREFORE) CLOSER TO *GOD...*

Z·P!

...A SO-CALLED *"NOBLE SAVAGE!"*

AH·AAAAAHHH!

84

THOMAS JEFFERSON WAS THE NOBLE SAVAGE *INCARNATE!* HE WAS BORN IN *1743* ON THE *EDGE* OF SETTLED VIRGINIA!

HIS UPWARDLY MOBILE FATHER *INSISTED* ON GIVING HIM A *CLASSICAL EDUCATION* WITH AN EMPHASIS ON *ENLIGHTENMENT PHILOSOPHY.*

GREEK PHILOSOPHY

FROM HIS ISOLATED RURAL *PLANTATION,* MONTICELLO -- THE HOUSE HE *DESIGNED* FOR HIMSELF -- JEFFERSON FOUND TIME TO --

Vote
☐ Yeh
☐ Nay

MAINTAIN A *LEGAL* PRACTICE

SERVE IN THE VIRGINIA *LEGISLATURE*

INVENT A *LAP DESK* AND AN IMPROVED *PLOW*

BECOME AN ACCOMPLISHED *VIOLINIST*

AND AMASS OVER 6,400 *BOOKS,* WHICH WOULD SERVE AS THE *BASIS* FOR THE *U.S. LIBRARY OF CONGRESS!*

JEFFERSON'S ENTIRE *LEGISLATIVE CAREER* INVOLVED FREEING THE COLONY'S CITIZENS TO FIND THEIR *OWN* INNER NOBLE SAVAGE!

HE *WROTE* THE STATUTE GUARANTEEING VIRGINIANS' *RELIGIOUS FREEDOM* TO FIND GOD IN *THEIR OWN WAY!*

GOD
(NO MENUS)

WORLD'S GREATEST EVERYTHING

~*SNORT!*~ HUH? WHA..?

I'M *SO* GLAD THE *MEDIEVAL EUROPEAN* SYSTEM OF *PRIMOGENITURE* MAINTAINS AN *AMERICAN* ARISTOCRACY BY FORCING *ALL LANDS* TO BE INHERITED BY THE *ELDEST SON -GAK!!*

BELIEVING THIS SYSTEM *UNNATURAL* TOO, JEFFERSON SPEARHEADED *ENDING* IT, SO *ALL* WOULD HAVE THE OPPORTUNITY TO *WORK THE LAND!*

YOU CAN ONLY *IMAGINE* HOW HE FELT ABOUT THE *BRITISH* ARISTOCRACY, WHICH *RULED* AMERICA FROM *LONDON!*

HE WAS ONE OF THE *FIRST* REVOLUTIONARIES TO OPENLY ADVOCATE *FULL* SUCCESSION FROM ENGLAND, IN 1774!

FOR THE DECLARATION OF INDEPENDENCE JEFFERSON TURNED IN SOME OF THE CATCHIEST *AD SLOGANS* FOR *DEMOCRACY* IN *HISTORY!*

BUT HE WAS NO *HIPPIE*. "PURSUIT OF HAPPINESS" HAD A VERY *SPECIFIC* MEANING TO SOMEONE OF HIS *CLASS...*

...IN JEFFERSON'S MIND AMERICA WAS TO BECOME AN *AGRARIAN PARADISE* DOMINATED BY *FARMER-INTELLECTUALS!*

THEM *V.R. GOGGLES* RUNNIN' ON TH' *COLD FUSION REACTOR* THAR, PA?

YESSUM. INVENTED THE GOL-DANGED THING AFTER I MILKED THE *HOG*, I DID.

POTATOES

YOU MEND THE *CHICKEN COOP* AND FINISH THAT MONOGRAPH ON THE NATURAL RIGHTS OF *PROPERTY* YET?

ALL IN ITS OWN GOOD *TIME*, MOTHER ...

IN OTHER WORDS, IF LEFT TO THEIR OWN DEVICES, *ALL* AMERICANS WOULD *NATURALLY* TURN OUT JUST LIKE *JEFFERSON!*

THERE WAS ONLY ONE SLIGHT *PROBLEM* WITH THIS PLAN, HOWEVER.

WHAT ABOUT *US*?

JEFFERSON WASN'T ENTIRELY "*JEFFERSON*" *HIMSELF!*

HIS "*NATURAL*" EXISTENCE WAS LARGELY A RESULT OF A *MAN-MADE* CONSTRUCT--ONE OF THE MOST *HEINOUS* IN HISTORY!

ABOUT *200 AFRICAN SLAVES* DID ALL OF JEFFERSON'S FARMING FOR HIM, GRANTING HIM THE *LUXURY* TO LIVE A LIFE OF THOUGHT AND SCIENCE!

FREEDOM

HOW TO *RECONCILE* SUCH AN *OBVIOUS* CONTRADICTION BETWEEN *IDEAL* AND *REALITY?*

"ALL MEN ARE CREATED EQUAL"

EASY...

NOT MEN

HEY! QUIT IT!

"...NEGROES ARE NOT *MEN!*"

BETTER PULL UP A *CHAIR.* SOMETHING TELLS ME YOU'RE GONNA BE *STUCK* HERE UNTIL THE *1960'S.*

HA! YOU'RE NOT SO TOUGH *NOW,* ARE YA, MR. "I'VE-GOT-OPPOSABLE-THUMBS!"

"IN **REASON** (BLACKS ARE) MUCH **INFERIOR**... **NEVER** COULD I FIND THAT A BLACK HAD UTTERED A THOUGHT ABOVE THE LEVEL OF PLAIN **NARRATION**."*

PRETTY **SIMPLE**, RIGHT?

*: T.J., *NOTES ON THE STATE OF VIRGINIA* (1783)

JEFFERSON'S **REAL** GENIUS LAY NOT JUST IN HIS **IDEAS** - BUT IN HIS ABILITY TO **CONVEY** THEM IN EASY-TO-UNDERSTAND TERMS! HE SAW ALL CONFLICTS AS STARK **WHITE** VERSUS **BLACK**!

(IF YOU'LL PARDON THE TERM.)

THIS **ACCESSIBILITY** OF HIS PHILOSOPHY HAS INSPIRED WOULD-BE **REVOLUTIONARIES** OF **EVERY** STRIPE EVER SINCE!

A T-SHIRT WITH **THIS** QUOTATION WAS FOUND IN THE APARTMENT OF OKLAHOMA CITY BOMBER **TIMOTHY McVEIGH**:

"The tree of liberty must be refreshed from time to time with the blood of patriots and tyrants."

— Thomas Jefferson

HE PROVED MUCH MORE ADROIT AT FIGHTING **BAD** LAWS THAN SUPPORTING **GOOD** ONES.

IRONICALLY, AMERICA'S GREATEST POLITICAL THEORIST **MISSED** THE ENTIRE **CONSTITUTIONAL DEBATES** SERVING AS THE USA'S AMBASSADOR TO FRANCE!

THERE HE DISTURBED MANY OF HIS COMRADES WITH HIS UNEQUIVOCAL SUPPORT OF THE BLOOD-SOAKED *FRENCH REVOLUTION*:

"RATHER THAN IT SHOULD HAVE *FAILED*, I WOULD HAVE SEEN HALF THE *EARTH* DESOLATED!"

BY THE MIDDLE OF HIS FIRST TERM AS *PRESIDENT*, JEFFERSON HAD MADE MANY *ENEMIES*, WHO THOUGHT HE WAS A *DANGEROUS RADICAL*. IN 1802 THEY SPREAD REPORTS THAT ALLEGED:

PRESIDENT JEFFERSON KEEPS ONE OF HIS *OWN SLAVES* AS HIS *MISTRESS!*

FRIGGIN' *ATTACK ADS...*

IN 1998, *DNA TESTING* ON DESCENDANTS PROVED THAT *SALLY HEMINGS*, A SLAVE 20 YEARS JEFFERSON'S JUNIOR, WAS HIS *LOVER* FOR *DECADES!*

JEFFERSON'S YOUNG WIFE HAD DIED IN 1781. RIGHT BEFORE THE *END*, SHE MADE HIM *PROMISE*:

YOU MUST *NEVER* ... MARRY ... AGAIN!

AND HE *DIDN'T.*

BUT JEFFERSON WAS **38** - NOT EXACTLY **CHASTE WIDOWER** MATERIAL - AND HE A PARTICULARLY **POIGNANT** TEMPTATION LIVING RIGHT UNDER HIS **ROOF**:

JEFFERSON **INHERITED** SALLY HEMINGS AND **99 OTHER** SLAVES FROM HIS WIFE'S **FATHER**. SALLY'S MOTHER, **BETTY**, WAS JEFFERSON'S **FATHER-IN-LAW**'S MISTRESS...

...SALLY WAS JEFFERSON'S **DEAD WIFE'S HALF-SISTER!**

WAS THIS A WAY OF HAVING HIS CAKE AND EATING IT TOO ... DID KEEPING AN ALLEGED **INFERIOR** AS HIS LOVER "NOT COUNT" AS BREAKING HIS PROMISE TO HIS WIFE?

OH YEAH! **NOW** YOU'RE TALKIN'!

AFTER ALL, THIS **IS** THE SAME MAN WHO TRIED TO BE A **SLAVEHOLDING** GURU OF PERSONAL FREEDOM!

"NOTHING IS MORE CERTAINLY WRITTEN IN THE BOOK OF **FATE**, THAT THESE PEOPLE (BLACKS) ARE MEANT TO BE **FREE**..."

"...NOR IS IT **LESS** CERTAIN THAT THE TWO RACES **CANNOT** LIVE IN THE **SAME** GOVERNMENT!"**

: T.J., **AUTOBIOGRAPHY (1821)

DESPITE HIS **RACISM**, JEFFERSON BELIEVED SLAVERY WAS **WRONG**-- YET IT WAS THE ONE **UNNATURAL** CONSTRUCT HE COULD **NOT** SLAY.

HIS ORIGINAL DRAFT OF THE **DECLARATION OF INDEPENDENCE** CONTAINED A PASSAGE **CONDEMNING** SLAVERY, BUT IT WAS EXCISED AT THE DEMAND OF **SOUTHERN DELEGATES!**

SLAVERY

WHEN HE WAS A YOUTHFUL MEMBER OF THE VIRGINIA LEGISLATURE, JEFFERSON INTRODUCED A BILL **ABOLISHING** SLAVERY, BUT IT WAS VOTED DOWN!

PERPETUALLY IN **DEBT** AFTER THE REVOLUTION, HE WOULD HAVE BEEN **RUINED** IF HE FREED HIS **OWN** SLAVES -- WHICH, AS PROPERTY, COULD BE USED FOR **EQUITY!**

-HEH-... SORRY ABOUT THIS GUYS... -GULP!-

IN GOD WE TRUST · LIBERTY · 1942

HE DEALT WITH HIS FAILURES AND CONTRADICTIONS BY *IGNORING* THEM! SLAVERY ... INFIDELITY ... THESE HAD *NO* PLACE IN HIS BLACK-AND-WHITE WORLD, SO HE *DEFERRED* CONFRONTING THEM *INDEFINITELY!*

LA-LA-LA, I CAN'T *HEAR* YOU...

SLAVERY *BLINDED* HIM TO AMERICA'S *TRUE* DESTINY-- WHICH WAS *INDUSTRIAL* AND *URBAN*, NOT PASTORAL AND AGRARIAN.

!%@#$!

AMERICA'S DEFERRAL OF THE *SLAVERY* ISSUE *EXPLODED* WHEN SLAVEHOLDING STATES TRIED TO *SECEDE* FROM THE UNION...

...QUOTING *JEFFERSON* AS JUSTIFICATION FOR THEIR *REBELLION*, OF COURSE.

AS INSPIRING AS JEFFERSON'S *WORDS* WERE, IT WOULD BE THE *BLOOD* SPILLED DURING THE *CIVIL WAR* THAT WOULD AT LAST REALIZE HIS *VISION* OF EQUALITY FOR *ALL*.

why you're WRONG

SECOND AMENDMENT EDITION

Well-Regulated Writing:
Fred Van Lente

Un-Infringed Art:
Ryan Dunlavey

color flats: *Stephen Meyer*

Whenever America has one of its periodic mass shootings, **sensible** people will say:

> WHY CAN'T WE KEEP THE **WRONG** PEOPLE FROM GETTING THEIR HANDS ON **GUNS?**

And you'll always get some **wise guy** who says:

> BECAUSE THE RIGHT TO HAVE GUNS IS IN THE CONSTITUTION!

> IT'S A **SACRED** RIGHT THAT CAN'T BE TAKEN AWAY! NOT FROM ANYONE! NOT FOR ANY REASON!

But **is** that what it says, **really?**

The text of the Second Amendment to the United States Constitution reads, in full:

A well regulated militia, being necessary to the security of a free state, the right of the people to keep and bear arms shall not be infringed.

Few sentences in the history of law have been so thoroughly agonized over.

But that's largely because some people really *want* it to mean things it *doesn't*.

Namely:

They want it to champion any *individual's* right to own *any* weapon he chooses.

But its references to *"well-regulated militia," "a state"* and *"the people"* (collectively) suggest otherwise.

Also:

Some want it to mean that it maintains the power of the *citizen* to counteract the power of the *state*, to keep it in line.

It is true that a major inciting factor for the American Revolution was the standing army Great Britain left behind in her colonies after she won the *French and Indian War*.

WE'RE HERE TO PROTECT YOU!!!

UH... THANKS?

Of course, the main reason Britain felt the *need* to do that...

...was because colonial *militias* performed so *terribly* during the war with France that the Empire learned they were a poor substitute for *professional* war-fighters.

Washington's Virginia militia surrenders at the Battle of Fort Necessity, 1754

Colonies formed local militias to defend against two primary threats:

Attacks by hostile *Native Americans* and *slave* rebellions.

In fact, many colonial laws made bringing weapons to public meetings like church services *mandatory* because large groupings of white people could be prime targets for *attack.*

Though citizen militias were a practical necessity for whites in the early colonial period, during the *American Revolution*, amateurs again proved *no match* for the pros.

Despite initial successes in the Boston area, the colonial militias got their *asses* consistently *kicked* by a well-trained, well-armed British/Hessian force.

THE FIGHTING'S *THAT* WAY!

WE KNOW! THAT'S WHY WE'RE GOING *THIS* WAY!

It was only once the militias were *"well-regulated"*— trained properly by sympathetic *European* officers— that they transformed into the *Continental Army*, able to stand up to the invaders.

GONNA *PUMP* YOU *UP!*

Nevertheless, the fear of the Continental Army becoming a tool of *tyranny* was very much in Congress's mind once the war ended in 1783.

So it was *disbanded* after the Revolution.

But problems with this arose almost immediately.

In 1786, Massachusetts farmers led by *Daniel Shay*, angry over debts and other grievances, attacked a U.S. armory in an attempt to overthrow the government.

Local merchants had to raise their own *"militia"* with private funds in order to stop the rebels.

UH... GUYS...

...I THINK WE'RE GONNA NEED A BIGGER *ARMY*...

Shay's Rebellion so freaked out the Federal government, then run by the weak *Articles of Confederation*, that they called for a new Constitution.

Ironically, yes, our *Constitution* was in part *inspired* by attempts of *individual citizens* to *overthrow the government!*

So it's not surprising that the Constitution provides no *"right to rebel,"* like a self-destruct switch in a mad scientist's laboratory.

On the contrary, the Constitution specifically prohibits treason, rebellion *and* insurrection and gives the government explicit power to combat these crimes by citizens.

FOOLS! THE SECRETS OF DEMOCRACY DIE WITH ME!!

GO BOOM

As is clear from the Constitutional debates themselves, the **Second Amendment** was added to imply that a standing army could be kept **small**-

-and therefore too **weak** to oppress the **people**-

-because it'd be **enhanced** in times of war by the **militias** that had been standard in the colonies for centuries.

Indeed, not long after the Constitution was ratified, when farmers took arms against the government again - this time in western Pennsylvania in 1791 - President George Washington did in fact raise such a *"national militia"* -

-- at **12,950 men** it was a bigger army than he at times commanded during the Revolution itself!

The *"Whiskey Rebellion"* dissolved before the national militia needed to fire a shot.

But increasing instability in Europe made the American government realize a **permanent military** was becoming increasingly necessary for national security.

As the British Empire had concluded before it, the U.S. decided there is no good **replacement** for **professional** warfighters.

(A *"militia navy"* doesn't really cut it, after all.)

So the idea of **militias** being an enhancement and **counter** to a professional army began to be **abandoned** before the 18th century even **ended**- **undermining** the whole point of the Second Amendment!

Granted, the idea remains in the state **National Guards** and other reserve forces.

But anyone who argues that the original purpose of the Second Amendment *wasn't* to support the *security* (not the overthrow) of the *state* (not the individual)–

A well regulated militia, being necessary to the **security of a free state**, the right of the people to keep and bear arms shall not be infringed.

–simply doesn't understand the history around the Constitution.

(And maybe doesn't read so good.)

It is telling that in the lobby of the HQ of the National Rifle Association they leave out the *militia/free state* part of the Amendment altogether!

"...the right of the people to keep and bear arms shall not be infringed."

The NRA and the gun manufacturers would very much like you to remain ignorant of this aspect of the debate.

So the next time someone gets in your face about this:

You can tell them:

why you're **WRONG**

THE BLOOD-RED SUMMER

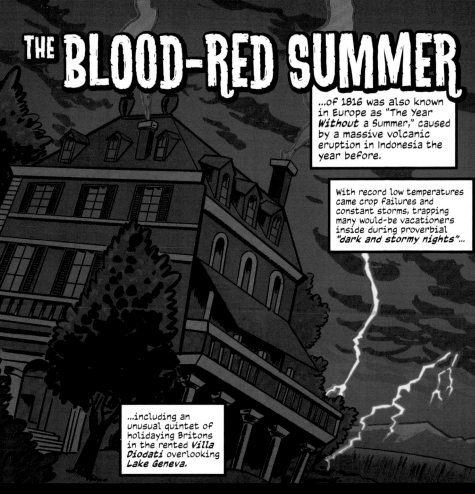

...of 1816 was also known in Europe as "The Year *Without* a Summer," caused by a massive volcanic eruption in Indonesia the year before.

With record low temperatures came crop failures and constant storms, trapping many would-be vacationers inside during proverbial *"dark and stormy nights"*...

...including an unusual quintet of holidaying Britons in the rented *Villa Diodati* overlooking *Lake Geneva.*

They wanted to enjoy hiking and boating, but instead were forced to entertain themselves.

They took turns reading aloud from a book of *German ghost stories*, but, finding them wanting...

...on the night of June 17, 1816, decided they could do *better*, daring each other to come up with the best *spooky tale.*

The actual renter was the hottest young poet in the world, *George Gordon, Lord Byron*, self-exiled to Switzerland after a series of sex scandals.

Byron's story was a muddied fragment about a traveling vampire, based on folktales he heard in Greece.

Dr. John Polidori was ostensibly Byron's personal physician, but was being paid by a London publisher to keep a journal of his travels with the poet.

His story was an updated Oedipus tale about a man who unknowingly sleeps with his own sister—the thing Byron very *knowingly* did that drove him from England.

Claire Clairmont was quite literally a Byron groupie. She had followed Byron to Geneva of her own accord after bedding him in an inn outside London.

Her story was about a lady who loses the flesh from her skull for peeping through a forbidden keyhole.

Unknown to most, she was currently pregnant with Byron's child.

To cement her insinuation into Byron's circle, Claire had dragged with her to Switzerland another hot young poet, *Percy Shelley*. He tried to tell a story from his childhood...

...but some quoted lines of Coleridge made him think of a female demon with eyes instead of nipples, a vision so horrifying he fled from the room!

Shelley had left his wife and child for Claire's slightly older stepsister, **Mary Godwin**, the beautiful daughter of two of England's most notorious social philosophers.

Mary struggled to come up with a ghost story of her own.

HEY, UH, MAYBE LET ME SLEEP ON IT, HUH?

WEATHER FORECAST SUCKS TOMORROW, TOO... HEH!

And her whole short life up until that point had been one of disappointing writers.

OOOH... GUESS THAT MEANS IT'S MY TURN, HUH?

Her father, **William Godwin**, was a social radical who equated marriage in his *Enquiry Concerning Political Justice* (1793) as tantamount to slavery.

But when Mary decided to put some of Godwin's theories of free love into practice by hooking up with Percy, one of her dad's biggest admirers, at age 17, he was...not pleased.

YOU WERE SUPPOSED TO BE A NEW KIND OF WOMAN!

BUT YOU GOT *KNOCKED UP* BY THE FIRST GOOD-LOOKING BAD BOY YOU MET!

YOUR MOTHER WOULD BE ASHAMED!! I'M SO GLAD SHE'S NOT ALIVE TO SEE THIS!!

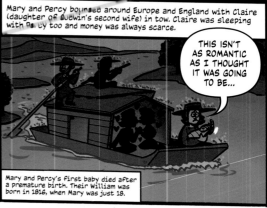

Mary and Percy bounced around Europe and England with Claire (daughter of Godwin's second wife) in tow. Claire was sleeping with Percy too and money was always scarce.

THIS ISN'T AS ROMANTIC AS I THOUGHT IT WAS GOING TO BE...

Mary and Percy's first baby died after a premature birth. Their William was born in 1816, when Mary was just 18.

William's rejection hurt Mary deeply. He had tried to raise her by the feminist principles of her mother, Mary Wollstonecraft, who died a few days after giving birth to her.

She learned her letters off the gravestones in the churchyard where the pioneering philosopher was buried.

100

MARY WOLLSTONECRAFT

(1759-1797) was born into a financially *shaky* middle-class English family. She spent her *teenage* years defending her mother from her father's *drunken rages*.

Disgusted by the lack of *employment opportunities* available to women, she resolved to become a *professional writer*... a nearly *unheard* of job for a woman in the 18th century. She declared:

"I AM THE *FIRST* OF A *NEW GENUS!*"

She scored her *biggest* success with 1792's *Vindication of the Rights of Women*, which attacked the assertions of thinkers like *Rousseau*...

>OOF!<

BOARD of EDUCATION

...who said that women should *only* be educated to be made good *companions* for *men*.

The *justification* of the time was that women were *silly* and *sentimental*, but Mary turned this assertion on its *ear*, asserting women acted this way *because* of their lack of education.

She wrote that women could be *better* companions to men--and better contributors to *society*--if their *reason* was developed in school along with their *"feminine"* qualities!

Therefore, in addition to being a seminal figure of *feminism*, in arguing that *society* constructed *"nature"* (as opposed to the other way around) she was a harbinger of *structuralism* as well!

Mary had a *tough go* trying to find her *own* perfect companion. While in *Paris*, she fell in love with an *American adventurer* who *rejected* her.

She tried to *kill herself* by jumping into the *Thames*, but bystanders rescued her. She went on to marry freethinker and anarchist *William Godwin*... but *died* giving birth to her second child, *Mary*.

Mary Godwin's many ghosts followed her to bed on the night of June 17, 1816. Years later, she'd write:

"When I placed my head on my pillow, I did not sleep, nor could I be said to think.

"I saw the pale student of unhallowed arts kneeling beside the thing he had put together.

"His success would terrify the artist; he would rush away from his odious handiwork, horror-stricken.

"I saw the hideous phantasm of a man stretched out, and then, on the working of some powerful engine, show signs of life, and stir with an uneasy, half vital motion.

"He would hope that, left to itself, the slight spark of life which he had communicated would fade...

"...that this thing, which had received such imperfect animation, would subside into dead matter.

"He sleeps; but he is awakened.

"He opens his eyes; behold the horrid thing stands at his bedside, opening his curtains, and looking on him with yellow, watery, but speculative eyes."

"I opened mine in *terror.*"

"The idea so possessed my mind, that a *thrill of fear* ran through me, and I wished to exchange the ghastly image of my fancy for the realities around."

Mary's subconscious had been fed by a number of sources that summer. Shelley and Byron argued over *science* and *philosophy*, in those days still largely *indistinguishable.*

The poets wondered whether *life* would be a *force* that would soon be identified along with electricity or oxygen, and all the others discovered over the last century.

Mary knew Italian physician Luigi Galvani had been able to make the parts of dead frogs move by stimulating them with an *electrical current.*

In 1803, Galvani's nephew hooked up a recently executed murderer to a giant *Voltaic pile* of 240 plates and zapped him into opening one eye!

Earlier in their travels, she and Shelley had passed by a *Frankenstein* Castle overlooking Darnstadt, Germany.

The name stuck to her tale, which thrilled her Lake Geneva companions, on the night of June 18th, 1816. Mary's husband encouraged her to expand it into a novel.

Though Mary is often identified with *Victor* Frankenstein, due to her difficulties as a *creator of life*—

—in many ways she can be much more strongly identified with the *Monster*,* created by then *rejected* for living out the free love, anarchic ideas of her philosopher parents!

DAILY NEWSY TIMES

TEEN MOM INVENTS SCI-FI

PAGE 2

* Mary Wollstonecraft refers to the aristocracy itself as "an artificial monster" in her *Vindication of the Rights of Men* (1790).

She subtitled *Frankenstein* "a Modern *Prometheus*," after the Titan who defies the gods and creates humanity from clay.

Percy got a publisher to bring the novel out *anonymously* in 1818. Despite a glowing review by *Sir Walter Scott*—who thought *Percy* wrote it— the first edition only sold 459 copies.

By contrast, Dr. Polidori ripped off Byron's story into *The Vampyre* (1819), which defined the modern archetype of a sexy, aristocratic bloodsucker, and became an *instant hit*.

Like Mary, Polidori's story was first attributed to somebody more famous— *Byron* himself, whom the titular vampire is clearly *modeled* after.

Still, few of the storytellers of the Blood-Red Summer lived very long or happy lives **beyond** it.

Percy Shelley's abandoned wife **Harriet**, pregnant by another man, drowned herself in Hyde Park's **Serpentine** in 1816.

HARRIET S. 17?? - 1816

This freed Percy to wed his current girlfriend, and at the end of that year Mary **Godwin** officially became Mary **Shelley**.

SHELLEY(s)

Dr. John Polidori, broke and depressed, drank cyanide and died in his father's house in 1821.

The couple moved to Italy, where Mary gave birth to **Percy Florence**, the only of her four children to live to adulthood.

Claire Clairmont gave birth to Byron's daughter, **Allegra**, whom Byron immediately took from her and gave to a Ravenna convent to raise.

POLIDORI

Claire was trying to convince the Shelleys to help **kidnap** her when the girl died of **scarlet fever** in 1822.

Two months later, Percy Shelley **drowned** with two friends in a storm off Tuscany.

ALLEGRA

SHELLEY P.

His rather theatrical **funeral** ended with his body being **burned** on a beach and an admirer refusing to give Mary his heart—which somehow **survived** the flames.

Lord Byron died of a sudden illness in 1824 helping Greek separatists against the occupying Ottoman Turks.

BYRON

Weirdly, though, one unexpected product of the summer of 1816 would enjoy a **rebirth** and (so far) **eternal** life.

It was *William Godwin*, of all people, who noticed stage adaptations of his daughter's novel had begun cropping up- and doing *whiz-bang business*.

The biggest hit was 1823's *Presumption, or the Fate of Frankenstein*, which followed a play of Polidori's *Vampyre* earlier that season.

But because *Frankenstein* was published *anonymously*, no one knew who to *credit* with the source material.

YOU HAVE DONE MY DAUGHTER A *GRAVE DISSERVICE*, SIR!

THE GUY'S A NUT! *RUN!*

BUT...I DON'T KNOW WHO YOUR DAUGHTER *IS!*

EXACTLY! THAT'S THE *PROBLEM!*

The success of the stage *Frankensteins* allowed Godwin to secure a new edition of the novel-with its true author's *full name* at last prominently on the cover!

THAT'S MY *BABY!* *SNIFF!*

Of course *"Frankenstein"* has entered the world's lexicon as shorthand for *any* well-meaning creation run amok with unintended consequences.

And Mary Shelley, who was 18 years old when she began the novel and 20 when it was published, became the *mother* of a whole new genre of speculative fiction.

106

And, if nothing else, *Frankenstein* reconciled William Godwin with his *own* misbegotten creation.

YOU'D STILL *LOVE* ME EVEN IF I DIDN'T WRITE A *GOOD BOOK*, WOULDN'T YOU, FATHER?

BUT NOW I DON'T *HAVE* TO!

Mary Shelley left London a scandal-plagued *Bohemian*; she returned a renowned and respected *woman of letters*.

She was able to attend a performance of *Presumption* herself in August 1823.

"BUT LO AND BEHOLD! I FOUND MYSELF FAMOUS!"*

MAMA! MAMA! WHY ARE WE CLAPPING? IS THIS YOUR STORY?

* Paraphrasing her pal Byron

YES, PERCY. *ONE SUMMER* A FEW YEARS BACK, YOUR FATHER AND I WERE IN A CONTEST TO SEE WHO COULD WRITE THE *BEST SCARY STORY.*

MAMA! MAMA! COME HERE!

I THINK YOU *WON.*

Cover art for *ACTION PHILOSOPHERS GIANT-SIZED THING* volume 2 (collecting issues 4-6 of the series), - self-published by Fred Van Lente and Ryan Dunlavey in 2006.

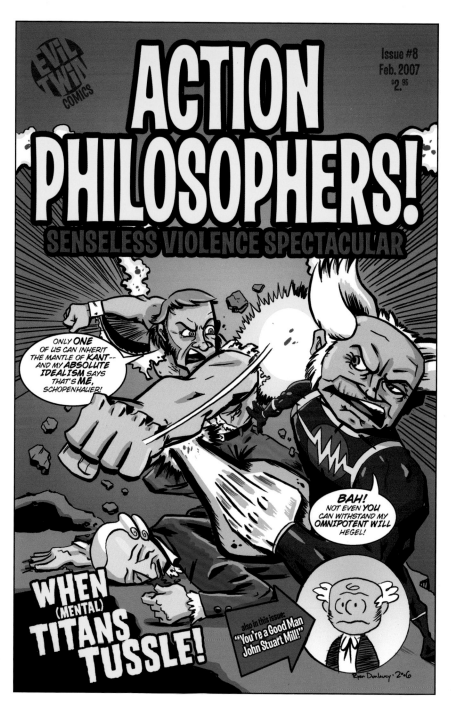

Cover art for ACTION PHILOSOPHERS #8 - self-published by
Fred Van Lente and Ryan Dunlavey in 2007.

About the Creators

Fred Van Lente Fred Van Lente (writer, research, lettering) is the #1 New York Times Bestselling, Harvey Award-Nominated writer of too many comics to count, including *Incredible Hercules*, *Marvel Zombies*, *Archer & Armstrong*, *Weird Detective*, *The Comic Book History of Animation*, *The Comic Book History of Comics*, *The Comic Book Story of Basketball*, and the *Action Activists* and *Action Presidents* series. He's also written three prose mystery novels, *Ten Dead Comedians*, *The Con Artist* and *Never Sleep*.

Ryan Dunlavey (artist) is the artist of *Action Activists*, *Action Presidents*, *The Comic Book History of Animation*, *The Comic Book History of Comics* (all co-created with Fred Van Lente), *Dirt Candy: A Cookbook* (with Amanda Cohen), the Eisner Award nominated *The Illustrated Al* (with "Weird" Al Yankovic), and lots more, probably. He really needs a nap.

Adam Guzowski (colorist) has colored comics for IDW, Image Comics, Red 5, and Boom Studios and (according to Fred and Ryan) he totally kicks ass.